SHAKARA:
dance-hall queen

Second Edition

Osonye Tess Onwueme

SHAKARA:
dance-hall queen

a play
by

Osonye Tess Onwueme

AFRICAN HERITAGE PRESS
NEW YORK · LAGOS · LONDON
2006

AFRICAN HERITAGE PRESS

NEW YORK   LAGOS
PO BOX 1433   PO BOX 14452
NEW ROCHELLE   IKEJA
NY 10802   LAGOS
USA   NIGERIA

TEL: 718-862-3262
FAX: 718-862-1440
EMAIL: afroheritage9760@aol.com
www.africanheritagepress.com

First Edition, African Heritage Press, 2000

Library of Congress catalog number: 2006937452
Onwueme Tess

Distributors: African Books Collective,
                  www.africanbookscollective.com

African Heritage Press is an affiliate of African Books Collective, (ABC), PO Box 721, Oxford OX1 9EN, UK

Cover Design: **African Heritage Press**

Selections: 2006

Drama, African Drama, African Literature, Gender Studies, Ethnic Studies, Multicultural Studies, African American Literature, Theatre.

ISBN: 978-0-9790858-1-9
ISBN: 0-9790858-1-0

ACKNOWLEDGMENTS

My students Eddy Kaiser and Sharon Bejin contributed immensely to the editing of this second edition of the play. For totally immersing themselves in the challenge of the task, I cannot thank them enough.

Fondly for my sons—

Kenolisa Amaechi
and
Bundo Osemuchèè—

My Gift

For Life

OTHER BOOKS BY THE AUTHOR

NO VACANCY (2005)
WHAT MAMA SAID (2003)
THEN SHE SAID IT! (2002) ***
SHAKARA: DANCE HALL QUEEN (2000) ***
WHY THE ELEPHANT HAS NO BUTT (2000)
TELL IT TO WOMEN (1997) ***
THE MISSING FACE (1997)
THREE PLAYS (1993)
LEGACIES (1989)
THE REIGN OF WAZOBIA (1988) *
MIRROR FOR CAMPUS (1987)
BAN EMPTY BARN & OTHER PLAYS (1986)
THE DESERT ENCROACHES (1985) ***
THE BROKEN CALABASH (1984) *
A HEN TOO SOON (1983)

*** *Award-Winning plays.*
* *Plays adapted into film*

CHARACTERS

SHAKARA:
A 17 year-old girl who resents her impoverished family and seeks recognition in the street among her gangster-friends who crown and name her the "Dance-Hall Queen.."

OMESIETE:
The middle-aged single mother of KECHI and SHAKARA. After years of service as MADAM KOFO's nanny, she currently serves as her laborer and tenant.

KECHI:
SHAKARA's 19 year-old sister and a self-proclaimed "Born-Again Christian."

MADAM KOFO:
The flamboyant 47 year-old landlady and drug baroness. She is OMESIETE's employer and DUPE's single parent.

DUPE:
SHAKARA's friend and MADAM KOFO's 17 year-old daughter, who detests her mother. Like her friend, SHAKARA, the rebellious teenager drifts into the streets.

UNCLE SHANKA:
A middle-aged Undercover-Agent and Divisional Police Officer. He plays the role of the wealthy semi-literate drug-baron, CHIEF CHAIRMAN, alias, Money-Miss Road.

SHOW BOY ONE & TWO:
The CITY-HOODLUMS who play the role of DUPE's boyfriend PRINCE, POLICE OFFICER, POLICEMAN ONE & TWO, DRIVER and the GUARD/ALAWO.

SETTING

All actions take place in a city that is sharply split between the exclusive suburban rich neighborhood and the impoverished ghetto/slum. In the play, OMESIETE's "bacha" or shanty and MADAM KOFO's mansion mark this split.

A NOTE TO THE DIRECTOR

Through the various stages of the play - especially in the flashback scenes - the characters play double roles. Directors should feel free to adapt the appropriate music, song, dance, props, setting and language familiar to the relevant context/audience. Note that the music, song and dance function as heightened integral stages of dialogue and not as mere incidents in the drama.

THE FIRST STAGE

Foreplay

(A cloudy morning in the heart of the metropolis, with traditional Juju or Folk Music in the background dominated by a small 'Bacha' or 'Shanty' in advanced stages of disrepair. A struggling coconut tree, anchored as if it holds the very life and root of the shanty's foundation stands, defying the nagging poverty all around it. Beneath this coconut tree are pieces and piles of firewood marked "Wood Chips For Sale." A tree stump marks each side of the shanty's boundary. As the stage opens, DUPE (in a local tie-dye top and jeans) appears agitated, standing one foot in, one foot out, and clinging to the rickety door-knob. She anxiously waits for SHAKARA who is in no hurry to finish her make-up. In her red-hot pants suit, SHAKARA sits on the tree stump opposite her friend and starts mounting her altar/shrine of cosmetics: lipsticks, mirrors, bleaching creams, soaps, pressed powder, a blonde wig and sexy fashion magazines glazed with erotic cover-pictures of sexy models that she is obsessed with. Now and again, SHAKARA holds up a mirror to her own face, sighs, and starts scrubbing and lifting or pinching her face and body with mixed bleaching cream, her wide nose into a cute "v". The boom-box sitting at her side bellows the latest Rap Music – loud enough to offend anyone who doesn't like that kind of music – until she steps into the latest youthful dance steps of the day: the Electric Shock, Break Dancing, Moonwalk, Boody Call, and Cry Babe. Finally, SHAKARA step-dances into the shack and returns with a red hot curling iron that she runs through her short, thick black hair. Her hair stubbornly protests, sizzles, hisses, and bounces back with a twang that leaves it no other choice but to kiss SHAKARA's ear. She jumps, crying out loud: "Damn it! This thing wan kill me-o!" Quickly, she

1

dabs the scorched ear with some gel from her make-up altar. DUPE is amused and finally snatches the hot iron from SHAKARA. She throws it into a corner and crosses the room to scoop some water to cool the iron. SHAKARA regains her composure and appears unconcerned with her friend's efforts as she now lifts her blonde wig, sprays it, and mounts it on her head before stepping into her erotic dance movements once more.)

DUPE: *(Irritated.)* Stop! *(SHAKARA ignoring her.)* Won't you stop?

SHAKARA: Girl, I'm the sole author of my life. Nobody rules it.

DUPE: *(Laughing.)* You? A mere brat? Competing with God? Ha! You and my mother. You'll never learn.

SHAKARA: Leave that woman alone. What is there to learn?

DUPE: A lot, my friend. The hot comb spoke it loud and clear. Listen!

SHAKARA: *(Dismissing her with a wave of the hand.)* Girl-friend, you're letting them cripple you. Yeah! You've been infected with that moral epidemic. *(DUPE replies with mock laughter. SHAKARA resumes her erotic dance.)* I am free. What does prophet Marley say? *(Sings.)* "Don't let them fool yah!"

DUPE: Great girl! Clap for the dreamer! Yeah, great dreamer! Ride on! *(Applauding.)* Ride on sistah! To the tide! Fire! But know they gonna get yah!

SHAKARA: I live by the Eleventh Commandment.

DUPE: *(Reciting.)* "Thou shalt not be found out." *(Pause.)* Oh ye fools! Wait until you get caught...in the net. *(Another round of applause with loud laughter.)*

SHAKARA: Laugh as you like. I know who I am.

DUPE: Yeah! The wanna-be!

SHAKARA: Nonsense!

DUPE: Precisely!

2

SHAKARA: You doubt where I am going? I know...

DUPE: Mad girl. Just keep on frying your hair. *(To the audience.)* My people, doesn't she look like a rat that's fallen into oil? Pitiful child! One of those who want to run before they can even learn to walk. Eh?

SHAKARA: I have to.

DUPE: *(Sternly.)* No, you don't!

SHAKARA: I need to. I am...fr...free. *(Sing-song manner.)* I am born to be...*(Humming.)* Free - Free - Free!

DUPE: Hey, freedom-child! Run! Fly! Icarus! But mind you get burnt!

SHAKARA: No problem.

DUPE: Yeah, *Hakuna Matata*. No problem. A friend's job is to keep the other from drifting; running too far and getting lost.

SHAKARA: To me, a friend's job is to let the other be.

DUPE: Even when they're running on the wrong track?

SHAKARA: Their life. Let them be.

DUPE: I see. But remember Icarus.

SHAKARA: Icarus? That unfortunate European? What's that got to do with me?

DUPE: Heat. The sun. Fate. The flight to heights must be moderated. Controlled.

SHAKARA: *(Laughing.)* Look who's talking! The mother-sucker herself! Matricide! Matricide!

DUPE: I am who I am. Beware of heights. That's all. Good luck on your journey.

SHAKARA: *(Scrubbing, applying bleaching cream.)* Amen. I need it. I need every charm I can get.

DUPE: Like your face? Pink. Mixed Coke, Fanta, Orange, Sprite. Girl, you can't bleach out fate, you know!

SHAKARA: *(Parodying.)* "Try as much as you will, a dog's nose is a dog's nose. It's always...Black." That's what my mother says. *(Sighs.)* That woman. Backward. Very backward.

DUPE: Let her be. You with your color-complex.

SHAKARA: So what? It's my face. Not yours!

DUPE: When will you learn that you can't change any-thing?

SHAKARA: Everything changes. That's what our teacher says.

DUPE: Nothing changes. Only faces...masks. That's all.

SHAKARA: Everything changes.

DUPE: Oh, yes! They do!

SHAKARA: For better...

DUPE: For worse, dreamer!

SHAKARA: Just wait. Watch this one change. But I'm no dog.

DUPE: Then what are you? A goat?

SHAKARA: A leopard. I'm a leopard. See my spots? My paws?

DUPE: Go, wild cat! It's your type who dare to rape God.

SHAKARA: Only the brave try. We try, try and try. One needs faith to try, you know. That's courage...*core-rage*, my friend. Need a lot of it to dare. So congratulate me. Don't you know me no more? *(Jubilant.)* I'm the brave and sassy queen! *(Strutting.)* I'm *Shakara! The Dance Hall Queen!* Watch me. Watch me fly. Soars into the skies! Winner! I'm gonna make it. Ha, my Gondola night club. See me-see me-here-I come! *(She does some break-dancing steps.)*

DUPE: *(Snapping.)* Girl, I can't wait anymore. Let's go!

SHAKARA: *(In a falsetto.)* Just hold on, girl-friend! You know I'm waiting for my sugar-d. *(Strutting.)* I'll be done soon.

DUPE: You better be! A bloody waste of time.

SHAKARA: Who says?

DUPE: You know he won't come. Trust no man.

SHAKARA: Girl, what's your problem? You've turned into

4

one of those male-bashing...

DUPE: I don't care. And I don't have any reason to...

SHAKARA: Not even your father?

DUPE: Don't taunt me. You know I don't have...

SHAKARA: *(Chuckling.)* One of these days, he'll just appear. *(Giggling.)* Yes, the Angel Gabriel himself. And with your mother, the immaculate queen by his side?

DUPE: *(Infuriated.)* Stop! *(Pause.)* Shak, don't hurt me. I've told you I don't have...

SHAKARA: *(Still teasing.)* Okay. He's taken her, I know. Ha! Ha! Ha!

DUPE: Can't stand it anymore! See you at the club tonite. *(She tries to go but SHAKARA grips her.)*

SHAKARA: Okay. You win now. But where are you running to?

DUPE: Wherever. Anywhere. Girl, I'm tired of waiting.

SHAKARA: *(Snatching her purse and sitting on her favorite tree-stump to resume her self-adornment.)* You know you're stuck with me? See? I got your purse? (DUPE finally chuckles and settles beside her friend on the tree stump.)*

DUPE: Now here I am. Do with me what you will.

SHAKARA: *(Laughing.)* Girlfriend, I know what the problem is...Some...
body...somebody's sleeping with my girl...*(Crosses over, strokes DUPE's face and calls out.)* Hey, people! Somebody's girl's got a chronic itch. She needs a good hand...a strong hand, don't you think? You all can see I'm busy. Will somebody help? I need help. *(She waits for answers, then resumes her face-painting.)*

DUPE: Shak, when will you ever get serious?

SHAKARA: Ha! Too many dull serious people in the world already. Why be another?

DUPE: *(Turning to go.)* Then go on running your mouth like a broken water-pipe. I'm leaving. *(SHAKARA intercepts her, holds her as she continues the teasing.)*

SHAKARA: *(Sing-song.)* Something's eating up my girl. What's the matter, dear? Mommy? Don't you know the sign? 'Mom's busy; Take a number.' Ha! Ha! Ha! *(She takes a few seductive dance-steps.)*

DUPE: *(Trying to free up herself.)* Shak you're sick. You both are.

SHAKARA: So I'm not alone in this? Your Mom too? Then I'm blessed. Sick. The whole world is...

DUPE: Go, check it out. Have your ears checked. Or better still, your head. I could help with that, you know. I'll be here, waiting...If only to save you from...from... yourself. *(She chuckles, silence.)* When is Mama coming back? That woman works too hard. I just can't wait to see her.

SHAKARA: Why wait? Go join her in the plantation. After all, it's your sweet mother's. *(DUPE turns away in disgust. SHAKARA realizes this, but continues teasing her.)* Mommy's baby. Don't worry. I'm here. I got it. Milk. And if you start yapping and yelling again, you'll get the big stick in...

DUPE: *(Flaring up.)* Won't you stop? I've told you, it hurts.

SHAKARA: *(Caressing her.)* The stick or your mama?

DUPE: Can we change the subject, please?

SHAKARA: Yes, baby. I hear you. The milk's gone: Again. And baby's sad. Don't cry...baby-woman. Don't cry. *(Cajoling, courting her. In her usual seductive manner, she breaks into a popular reggae tune, as she dances: "No woman no cry." DUPE is amused and joins her in a duet as she combs and weaves SHAKARA's hair. Suddenly excited.)* Yes! I know what's eating you up! That's why you can't wait. Eh? The Prince! The Prince Charming! *(Turning to the audience.)* Fellow countrymen and women! Somebody's girl is an aspiring broken heart. Love-sick. Always. *(Loudly.)* Any doctor here? Help! Help! *(She waits for their responses.)* Girlfriend, take note: 'Before you meet your Handsome Prince, you have to kiss a lot of toads.' Got it?

DUPE: *(Vexed.)* As if it's all that matters!

SHAKARA: What else matters?

DUPE: Nothing.

SHAKARA: You lie. Money Matters!

DUPE: Your headache. Not mine.

SHAKARA: *(Hysterical.)* I know. Transfer it. I want it! I need it! I dig it! So help me, God. *(Singing.)* I want you! I need you...I...

DUPE: You know what you sound like? Like a resounding empty drum—just like that woman who calls herself 'mother.'

SHAKARA: Isn't it a gross miscarriage? You, too, you sound like mine. And worse still, like my 'holy' sister who's shrinking from daily work, fasting and praying until she disappears. *(Mock laughter.)* She's so proud of being a *Born-Again Christian*. And I'm so happy being a *Born-Again Pagan*! *(Pause, cuddles DUPE.)* Baby, think it over. You have it all. Choose.

DUPE: *(Sighing.)* Oh, how I wish!

SHAKARA: Sick. That's what you are...like everybody else around me. Otherwise how could anyone so blessed, feel so...so...

DUPE: Cursed! Say it. Yes, cursed!

SHAKARA: Cursed? By whom?

DUPE: My birth. My mother.

SHAKARA: A great woman. The envy of the world! Princess and jewel among her peers! The hand that mints money. Money? A curse? Maybe I'm a fool to think...

DUPE: As if you don't know.

SHAKARA: Then let me be...

DUPE: A fool in the making.

SHAKARA: No, "Certified." Yes, a "Certified Fool." That's what I am. *(Smiles.)* Minted with hard currency! Now you know why I adore your mother.

DUPE: *(Rising.)* Then go hug her! Take. Take her until you

both go ruin each other. And leave me alone. I'm leaving.

SHAKARA: *(Trying to restrain her.)* Why do you have to take everything so seriously. Nothing in life's worth it, you know. As if I love my own mother any more.

DUPE: My kind of woman...that woman. I love mine less...

SHAKARA: I love yours more.

DUPE: And I love yours more.

SHAKARA: I love mine much, much, much less.

DUPE: And mine much more?

SHAKARA: Yes. Then let's exchange.

DUPE: You have mine. Take her. And please, keep the change. All I want is to be a thousand miles away from that woman.

SHAKARA: I wish I could be near. *(Giggling.)* You have mine. But sorry. No change to take or keep. You know her. More wretched than a church-rat. Just nothing...to keep. What is there to keep in poverty? And in walking misery such as my mother? What is there to keep? Nothing, Dupe. So each day you wake up, count your blessings.

DUPE: My curse, you mean? *(Wry laughter.)* Girl, you don't know what you have until you lose it.

SHAKARA: Isn't that what they say? Ha! Losers! That's what they all say to comfort themselves. But I'm not going to go through life losing. *(Singing and swinging.)* No! I'm a winner! A born-winner! Up me! *(Strutting.)* And girl, you know what I did to that Sugar-Daddy at the Gondola night-club?

DUPE: Hey, ride on!

SHAKARA: What happens when the hunter gets hunted?

DUPE: *(In a sing-song manner.)* What happens-What happens?

SHAKARA: *(To the audience.)* Ever met a yeye sugar-daddy with the zipper problem?

8

DUPE: Show them!

SHAKARA: Let's show! *(A screen shows the girls play-acting the romantic scene between SHAKARA and the preying SUGAR-DADDY at the Gondola night-club. SHAKARA is 'dressed to kill' and poses dangerously by the corner of the bar, where she is peeling and sucking a banana as the hunter speaks with his talkative eyes. Here, DUPE plays the role of the drooling SUGAR-DADDY.)*

DUPE/SUGAR-DADDY: Honey, girl. I'm hungry.

SHAKARA: *(Seductively offering.)* You care for banana?

DUPE/SUGAR-DADDY: *(Grabbing it hastily.)* I want it. *(Tries touching her below.)*

SHAKARA: Hey, man! Stop trespassing! *(In Pidgin English or Jamaican Patois.)* That na me future, you know!

DUPE/SUGAR-DADDY: Your poos...?

SHAKARA: Yes! Me poos's...me future! *(Laughs.)* High Voltage area. Don't you dare!

DUPE/SUGAR-DADDY: *(Drooling.)* But I can handle...Anything. *(Tries to dive in again.)*

SHAKARA: *(Gripping her crotch.)* You want it for free? No way! Pay before service!

DUPE/SUGAR-DADDY: *(In Jamaican Patois.)* Stop naw! "Me haffi eat, you know. Anytin. Can't wait now wo—man!"

SHAKARA: *(Seductively offering the banana.)* Honey, I got what you need. Aid...

DUPE/SUGAR-DADDY: *(Grabs the offering).* Then give it to me! *(The SUGAR-DADDY is lost in his love chant and quickly empties his pockets before his mistress.)*

SHAKARA: *(Quickly collects her booty, falls for him.)* Money for hand?

DUPE/SUGAR-DADDY: Back na ground! *(Red lights as the famished lion devours his prey. Rapid groans of "Jeee! Jeee! Yesu-Yesu-Yesuuuuuuuh! Save!" Then the hunter roars: "Woman stop it! How can you be on top of Mohammed and be calling Jezuz? You drunk on Jezuz?" Silence. The girls end their role-play and burst into laughter.)*

9

DUPE: That's what you learnt in school?

SHAKARA: *(Suddenly irritated.)* Jargon. School's jargon. I can't stand. I'm sick and tired of that stuff.

DUPE: Sick? *(Laughing.)* I know what you're suffering from: *mourning...mourning sickness.*

SHAKARA: Not for me. I'm tired.

DUPE: Wired!

SHAKARA: I said tired! Wasted. What's the sue of all that school stuff when you have no penny in your pocket. Ehn?

DUPE: Knowing that you don't, but that you can. It's faith, you know.

SHAKARA: Nonsense! What is my faith worth?

DUPE: A promise.

SHAKARA: What can it buy? Can you take it to the bank?

DUPE: They say knowledge is the beginning of wisdom.

SHAKARA: Bull-sh...!

DUPE: Knowing is living. Life.

SHAKARA: Knowing is nagging. Pain. You know, like a toothache?

DUPE: It boils down to healing...

SHAKARA: You mean killing?

DUPE: Then we agree...

SHAKARA: To disagree...

DUPE: Same with my Mother.

SHAKARA: Strange bed-fellows we are. I kiss...

DUPE: And I spit. *(Chuckling.)* Strange how life gives you one thing when you want another?

SHAKARA: Then take it, *As Is.*

DUPE: That's what is called *Core-rage*! Ha! Ha! Ha!

SHAKARA: I need it.

DUPE: Let's move.

SHAKARA: *(Suddenly moody, she explodes.)* Don't taunt me!

Can't you see I'm stuck? Where in the world am I supposed to go...with nothing?

DUPE: *(Playfully pushing her.)* Then stay put, girl. I'm on my way. *(She turns to go. SHAKARA intercepts her.)*

SHAKARA: Where do you think you're going and leaving me here?

DUPE: Somewhere. You want to come along?

SHAKARA: Girl, you know I'm stuck with you.

DUPE: Then we're going nowhere!

SHAKARA & DUPE: *(Giggling.)* Until further notice! *(They wrap their hands around each other as they briefly rock and sing: Take my hand, precious lord. Lead me home. Let me stand. I'm tired, I'm weak, I'm worn...)*

SHAKARA: *(Calmly.)* Dupe, you know, I've been seeing your mother in my dreams lately?

DUPE: Still with that man?

SHAKARA: Which one? The Police Officer or the Chief Chairman?

DUPE: Both. Does it matter? She's with them all, anyway. And they're all vultures... hovering for dead meat. Remember that I already gave you my recipe. Run! Or you will be eaten like everything and everybody else around them. I tell you, I was born by a ghost.

SHAKARA: Your mother?

DUPE: And father!

SHAKARA: Your mother lives.

DUPE: And dies daily!

SHAKARA: She lives.

DUPE: *(Laughing.)* Living, she dies. Both. That woman is an apparition. Walking bad news! Run! Run for your dear life!

SHAKARA: Then why live with it...I mean...with her?

DUPE: Do I have a choice? Who is my father? Where is my father? At least you know yours even if he doesn't care. But for me? I wish...*(Sighs.)* Aaah! These accidents of birth! *(Pause.)* Girl, life's a bastard, offering you lemon...

SHAKARA: Then make lemonade!

DUPE: *(Teasing.)* Silly girl! You think it's that easy?

SHAKARA: I'll take a chance.

DUPE: *(Laughing.)* You chancer! Take all the chances in the world and get ready!

SHAKARA: *(Shaking herself provocatively.)* Ikebe super! Bottom power! *(They fall into each other's arms, swinging and dancing a few erotic dance-steps.)* Yes, I'm a leopard. Don't try to change my spots.

DUPE: For even God is not safe in your hands!

SHAKARA: *(Mock toasting.)* Then let's drink to that!

DUPE: But mind you drown!

SHAKARA: My luck.

DUPE: Enjoy it while it lasts. *(Clapping salute.)* Go, tell your Mama, Baby B...itch! Yeah!

SHAKARA: *(Stops, fascinated.)* Ah, cool! I like that. *(Strutting.)* From now on, call me the Baby B...itch! Yeah!

DUPE: The new star. Add that to your medallions!

SHAKARA: *(Posing.)* 'Sha-ka-ra: Dance Hall Queen.' Alias: 'Baby B...'

DUPE: Nobody else sees your break-lights. Ride on girl! I'm with you.

SHAKARA: 'Til your Mother comes?

DUPE: Until the Mother comes. Her Royal Highness, the Queen Mother...

SHAKARA: *(Cutting in.)* Just who's that? How blessed I'd be to meet such...such...*(Pause.)* Dupe, I need one, desperately. And since you know, won't you introduce me to her?

DUPE: Me? Who am I?

SHAKARA: Blessed.

DUPE: No Shak. It's you. Can't you see? Your Mother...the

Queen Mother herself?

SHAKARA: Who? My mother, a queen mother? *(She laughs into DUPE's face, then turns to the audience as she pokes her index finger into her head – indicating that her friend has gone mad. Meanwhile, DUPE stands apart, observing her friend with a mix of pity and incredulity.)* My girlfriend is suffering...I mean day-dreaming. Ha! In all these shards and broken pieces, she sees nothing but royalty. Ha! "Omesiete. Queen Mother of the Slums!" *(Pause.)* My people can't you see? The girl needs urgent help. *(Loudly.)* Help, people! The poor child is an emergency. I'm about to lose the only friend and family I have to acute madness. Will you help? *(SHAKARA steps into the shack. Now smiling, DUPE steps forward to the audience.)*

DUPE: Poor child. It's she who needs urgent help. Otherwise, how can anyone so rich, so blessed with the Queen Mother herself not know it? Eh, people? Think. You know, this reminds me of what the dog said: "Those who have buttocks don't really know how to use them. But those of us who don't, strain so hard to perch on our tails." Ha! *(Pause.)* But I tell you, right here in all these broken pieces of eh...well...I see the Queen Mother so close. My friend says I'm day-dreaming. Maybe. But you see this dress-top? *(She steps toward the audience, looks back to see if SHAKARA is within earshot, and tiptoes to shut the door before settling in the center-stage to tell her own story. Positions conspiratorially with the audience, but she is unaware that SHAKARA is already watching her from her tree stump.)* Shak never likes to hear this. So it's for your ears only! You know who gave me this dress-top? Her mother! I was seven years old. Kids playing, you know? Hide and seek. Monkeying from one tree to another? Well, it happened. A crack that left me with a broken arm for seven...eleven whole weeks! I cried: "Mooother!" But guess who was there to rescue me? Her mother, my nanny! *(Showing the top.)* She bound up my dangling arm with this! Her best wrapper, then. I spread it on my pillow every day I was in that hospital, and even after, until my mother began to protest. "Dupe, won't you get rid of that nonsense? Now here!" Then she'd smother me with many more expensive gifts to cover-up. But in spite of it all, I still clung to this piece of love. This faded piece of cloth that I finally made into a dress-top on my sixteenth birthday. And this she wants me to forget? For what? Just because she gave birth to me? Where was she when I needed her to nurse my wound? Gone! Nursing her precious weeds. Gone for her business, Career Woman! So what does she expect me to do? Fly or freeze? Ha, my friends! Love's not like tap water that you can turn on and turn off at will, you know? No! Like her mother, the Queen Mother said to me one day, "Love is a two-way traffic; of partners traveling, together." Make sense to you? Well, it does to me – the Queen Mother's "anthem of love." Now people, will you celebrate with me? Put your hands together for the "Queen Mother" herself! *(Rounds of applause.)* Another! And another! *(Suddenly, her mood changes. She stops the cheering audience and frowns.)* Now people, tell me. Who's a Mother? The one who gives birth, or the one who gives care? To me, Mother is – "The Care-Giver!" And what about you? What is Mother to you? Who's Mother to you? Tell me-tell me. This question's nagging-choking me. And I will not rest until I find the answer! So help me, friends, Where do I go from here? Until my queen, the real mother comes, I will be waiting. Yes, waiting... *(SHAKARA coughs in the doorway. Embarrassed, DUPE tries to cover-up with a smile.)*

SHAKARA: *(Cuddling her.)* You're just like me, eh? Poor baby! Don't worry. We're family. Come. Be mine! *(Pulls her towards the audience.)* My people. Meet Dupe. "Dupsy Dear" or "DD" for short. *(Caressing her.)* "DD" my friend. My mother. My father. My sister. My brother. My family. My...*(Smiles.)* Friends, home is not where you live, but a place that lives in your heart. For me, this is it: DD, my home. My life! *(Holding onto DUPE's chin.)* Isn't it wonderful, so wonderful to have someone who means the world to you? And so cute too? If there's any blessing...this is it! Got ya! *(Urging.)* Please clap for her! Again! Again! *(SHAKARA embraces her, then breaks into a popular tune: "Tonite is the night!" They exchange a clapping salute. Still singing and holding onto each other, they drift into the yawning streets. A screen projects them until the lights fade into the next scene. Two CITY HOODLUMS can be seen trailing, teasing and mocking them with highly provocative dance-steps as the girls are cursing and chasing them away.)*

THE SECOND STAGE

"A Mourning Sickness"

(KECHI enters carrying a basinful of yams. OMESIETE trails her, burdened with a heavy load of wood which she normally piles up for sale beneath the coconut tree. KECHI waits for her sister's help, but SHAKARA simply ignores her and continues with her make-up. KECHI stoops down, tries hard to bring down the load all by herself. Too heavy, the load tumbles; the yams break and scatter all around. SHAKARA giggles and quickly steps into the shack and turns on her loud music again as OMESIETE enters.)

OMESIETE: Is she gone again? *(No answer except for KECHI's groans. Looking out for her younger daughter who has disappeared, she calls.)* Nwaebuni! Nwaebuni! Where are you? *(No response. Seeing KECHI, groaning and nursing her bruised knee, OMESIETE quickly puts down her load to help soothe the wounded knee.)* You've fallen again? Kechi when? When will you learn to watch your steps? Ehn? Don't you know what it is like in this leaky hut? *(Searching.)* And so, where is that nasty sister of yours? Nwaebuni! *(Spotlight narrows on SHAKARA at the corner-stump as she is busy dancing, preening herself and repainting her nails. Loud laughter breaks through the radio, followed with a familiar tune. For a while, the music fills the atmosphere as OMESIETE hurries in and out of the shack to attend to KECHI and put things together before she resumes her search for SHAKARA.)* So where is that child? *(Sees her.)* Nwaebuni, are you deaf? Can't you hear me? Ehn? *(SHAKARA ignores her. OMESIETE is hysterical.)* Nwaebuni! So you won't answer me, Eh? *(Silence.)* What in the world are you doing when your only sister comes home with such a heavy load on her head, right in front of you? Is it too much to give a helping hand? *(Silence, except for KECHI's groaning.)* Well, any normal child would have done that—Help! Help! But, no. Not you, Nwaebuni. You have grown wings. Oh yes you have! And you now know what your mother knows, eh? *(No response.)* Ah ya-ya-yah! *(She breaks into mock laughter and clasps her hands furiously into SHAKARA's face.)* At seventeen? Ehn? Well, well, *One day monkey go go Market E no go come back.* One day...someday...you will learn. But it's not me...No! Not this poor Omesiete who will teach you the hard lessons of life that you so desperately need to bring you back to your senses. Ah ya-ya-yaaa! *(Mock laughter.)* We shall see...We shall see how the python basks in the sunshine! Ha! Ha! Ha! *(SHAKARA tries to block her ears with her index fingers. The mother is incensed, raises her voice and stands in her face threateningly. But SHAKARA turns away. KE-CHI is limping around and gathering the broken pieces of yams by the corner-stump.)* No Kechi. You've done enough already. Leave that alone and go take a bath.

KECHI: Yes, mother. *(KECHI exits. OMESIETE starts picking up the yam pieces.)*

OMESIETE: I should have known that I was only wasting my saliva talking to this deaf, wicked, arrogant child whose heart is made of stone. I should...have. *(Turning to SHAKARA.)* Otherwise how can anybody explain why you're filled with so much hatred for your own family? Ehn? Child, tell me. How can you remain in this place and let your own sister continue to suffer?

SHAKARA: I didn't send her to labor. Did I?

OMESIETE: *(To the audience.)* People of the world! Can you smell the trash from her mouth? My own daughter? *(Pause.)* Say that again and you will regret the very day you were born into this family.

SHAKARA: *(Stroking the wig on her head.)* As if I don't regret it already!

OMESIETE: *(Incensed.)* Now take off that ugly smelly thing on your head! You hear me? *(SHAKARA resists.)* I say take it off! *(Brief struggle until OMESIETE gives up and addresses the teenager calmly.)* Nwaebuni.

SHAKARA: *(Pouting.)* Haven't I told you to stop calling me that stupid name? *(Mimicking.)* Nwa-ebu-ni! Wa-ebu... Don't you dare call me that bush name again. I reject it!

OMESIETE: *(Mock laughter.)* Ha! Ha! Ha! Now tell me, you who haven't yet sold in the market and are already celebrating your profit. Eh? Tell me! Tell me what your name is! *(Grabbing the rebellious teenager, they struggle.)*

SHAKARA: Leave me! Let me go!

OMESIETE: Not until you tell me your name. "Acada!" Today you will tell me your name. I'm waiting. *(Still picking up the pieces of yam and wood that she piles under the coconut tree.)* Is this not the breast that suckled you? Is this not the womb that bore you? For you and your sister, I toil each day and night. Scratching the bare earth for a living. Look at the broken pieces! Yam-chips! That's all I have to sell to make a living for you and...(Voice cracking.)* Can't you see?

SHAKARA: You weren't forced to have me, were you?

OMESIETE: How can you talk to me like that? *(Restraining herself.)* Child, if...if only you knew...just what you mean to me...

SHAKARA: You're lying.

OMESIETE: Me lying? To you? When you are my life? *(She tries to draw near but SHAKARA keeps her distance.)*

SHAKARA: I don't need anyone to tell me that I'm an orphan. I know it. Nobody cares for me.

OMESIETE: For God's sake, don't be silly! Where did you get that idea from? Are you not my Ebuni? *(Cajoling.)* Tell me, do you know the meaning of Nwa...

SHAKARA: Stop right there! I know. You've explained that countless times and I'm so sick and tired of hearing you say that...(Parodying.)* Nwaebuni-Nwaebuni. *The child uplifts. Children uplift.* Uplift? With what? Empty-handed? Let's talk about something else, for I am just so sick of this place.

OMESIETE: *(Chuckling.)* Foolish girl! How can you know the meaning of it all...what life means to me...to us?

SHAKARA: *(Strutting.)* I don't know and don't want...My name is Shakara. And that's it!

OMESIETE: *(Mimicking her.)* See! See her! The half-naked "Queen of the Slums." The chicken plume which flies to the dance-floor even when the chicken is still at home. Fly! Fly high until those wings get broken. Only then you will know. Ha! *Sha-ka-ra: Queen Bluff! (Loud laughter.)* Whoever names herself that way? You senseless girl!

SHAKARA: I won it; my new name.

OMESIETE: Child, tell me, how does anyone win a name?

SHAKARA: Well, I did. And that's my name.

OMESIETE: *(Mock laughter as she tries a few break-dancing steps.)* To be crowned by those gangsters who get you spinning and spinning your tail like *koso?* Are you out of your mind? Ah, my poor child. I knew it. I knew they were going to lead you astray. And that's why I've been fighting and struggling. *(Cajoling.)* My dear child. You should know you're much more precious than all of them put together. My dear, you must go back to school. Stay away from them. Those riff-raff gangsters are nothing but trouble! Trouble! Trouble-O!

SHAKARA: Say whatever you like. I know myself...where I want to be. Those ones you label riff-raffs are the best family I ever have to give me hope. They crowned me. Named me the *Dance-Hall Queen.* Without them, what else do I have to my name? Nothing. And yes, my name is "Sha-ka-ra! Dance-Hall Queen." *(Strutting.)* I like me. I love myself!

OMESIETE: *(Amused.)* Foolish girl! You are truly out of your mind. Know this child; the old woman who sees a baby suckling, too, knows the taste of milk. Ha! My daughter! Like you now, I too was once a teenager; young, sexy, beautiful, psychedelic. *(Sighs.)* Ah, child! You want me to remember? No! Not now. Not now. Someday, maybe. But one thing I know for sure is that this "sassy" thing won't take you very far.

SHAKARA: *(Still strutting.)* You know where I go every night? Night clubs. Like the Nasty Girls. The Gondola. Caban Bamboo. Labamba...Where the green hard currency is...with the guys: Italian, Lebanese, French, American, English, Portuguese, Spanish...

OMESIETE: My poor child. Lost! Lost! You children of nowadays have no ears.

SHAKARA: We do.

OMESIETE: But you only wear them as mere decorations.

SHAKARA: At least we're doing something.

OMESIETE: *(Pulling.)* No, my babe. Come to me. I must talk to you.

SHAKARA: I have no time. I'm leaving any moment now. *(OMESIETE pulls up a bench, sits, while SHAKARA takes her favorite spot on the tree stump.)*

OMESIETE: *(Calmly.)* Let's sit here. There are many things I have to tell.

SHAKARA: *(Irritated.)* I got no time, Mama.

OMESIETE: *(Sternly.)* Then you must make time!

SHAKARA: I can't.

OMESIETE: Then, I'm going to make you...*(Confidential tone.)* Look, my dear daughter. I don't want you to make the same mistakes that I made in my youth. No. You need to learn from the past.

SHAKARA: There is nothing to learn.

OMESIETE: How do you know? Now listen. *(On the screen, "The Beast" – a Mercedes Benz 500 – cruises by. SHAKARA tries to run after it, but OMESIETE holds her back.)*

SHAKARA: *Struggling.)* Not now. Let me go. *(The Beast vanishes.)* You see what you have done?

OMESIETE: To save your life?

SHAKARA: *(Infuriated.)* To ruin it! Ruin my day! Can't you see? That's ready money that you just chased away! *(OMESIETE pulls her protesting daughter along to sit with her by the stump, then calls KECHI to join them.)*

OMESIETE: Children, hear me. For once, listen. *(Pause.)* How do you think I ended up like this? You think it was always hard like this? Like you now, I had great promise. Believe me, I did. But I ruined it. Ruined myself and here I am today. *(Voice cracking.)* You know...your father...?

SHAKARA: I don't know anything. And don't want to know.

OMESIETE: *(Sternly.)* Then somebody has to make you know. As my mother used to say, it is the duty of the old to let the youths know. And it is the duty of the youths to heed advice from the old. Note, too, that "if you pound well, you pound in the mortar. If not, you pound on the ground." But then, when I was young, like you now, I wouldn't listen. Well, look where I am; I slipped, and today, I'm still struggling.

KECHI: So Mother, tell us. What happened to you?

OMESIETE: *(Chuckling.)* You, my children...happened to me!

SHAKARA: Yes, pass the blame! There's always a scapegoat. And I am yours. Ha! Ha! Blame me for every failure in this God-forsaken place.

KECHI: Won't you let her speak!

SHAKARA: Am I talking to you? Miss Santa-Santa, Her Holiness, Queen of the Slum!

KECHI: *(Charging.)* And you?

OMESIETE: Hush! Hush children! *(Silence as the girls exchange wicked glares.)* Yes, my precious jewels. I'm not trying to...I mean...I cannot blame you for anything. But I do want you to learn from my own experience, what you may call failure.

SHAKARA: That's yours, not mine. I'm not here to inherit

anybody else's failure but mine. Don't you burden me with the past. Your past. Just like you now, let me have my own experience. Make my own mistakes. And besides, times have changed.

OMESIETE: For the worse!

SHAKARA: Who are you to judge? What do you know?

OMESIETE: *(Rising.)* Ah, sassy tongue! I know I'm nothing. But hear me. My duty as a parent is to tell you what you need to know. What you do with it is your own business! *(She calms down. Sits.)* You wonder why we're not with your father today?

SHAKARA: Well, you broke up.

OMESIETE: Why? You think any woman with children just wakes up one day, and decides to break up and walk away from years of marriage? With her children too? Ah, children! *(The mother sighs deeply as she turns to SHAKARA.)* What do you know about my past? And your father? *(Silence.)* I have always wanted to tell you, but will you listen? Your sister knows a lot.

SHAKARA: *(Rising.)* Then tell her the rest and leave me alone. *(OMESIETE quickly pulls her back to sit down.)*

OMESIETE: *(Emphatically.)* Li—sten! *Eneke-nti-mkp!* Listen to your mother! You deaf one, who sold your ears and bought wild eyes to look beyond your reach! Listen! "The fowl which refuses to listen hears inside the anus of the wolf." *(Silence. OMESIETE stands between the girls, takes both of their hands and pulls them towards the dwarf coconut tree to sit around it. She settles down to tell her story. SHAKARA is silently drawing and digging the mud with her big toe.)* Now my dear children. It is important for you to know me…where I'm coming from. That you may know why I am here now. *(She coughs, clears her throat.)* I was only sixteen, and he, sugar-coated tongue, some years older. Often, he would come monkeying around our compound. My mother saw this and warned me strictly to preserve myself and face my studies, for that was more important to her since she never had the opportunity to go to school herself. Despite my mother's warning, I turned a deaf ear to her and gave myself to this man that promised me the world. Why? Because he said that he loved me. He vowed it! I loved him too; at least so I thought. He promised that he'd love me forever. Take absolute care of me. And provide me with the money to start my own business. Ha! But then what did he do? Ha! Where are those promises now? In the drain. In the sand. Little did I know. See...now where I am? In the dump. *(Sighs.)* My sin? Love. I loved him. Let him devour me. He sucked me dry. Chewed...gobbled up my youth. And then spat me out. Once I had you, my children, I became irrelevant. An article without any value to the man I loved. After my second child, he started to avoid my bed and find faults. Many faults! My soup was no longer sweet. My food was too cold for his stomach that he'd not even touch it. He'd stay out late. Oh so late at night. Then come back tired and not want to do anything with me. And then one morning, he woke up and told me that he was relocating. He had found himself a wife. With my dream of school and a bright future aborted, what else was there for me? Children, that is why I am here, today. *(Pause.)* Do I blame anybody? No! Nobody but...myself...If...only I had listened to my mother! But God is kind. I have you...both to hold on to...*(Choking.)* See...now where I am. *(Pause.)* Ah ya-ya-yah! My children, if you really want to know, I think your father lost interest in me because he expected male children. But do I make children? Don't I take what God gives me? *(To SHAKARA.)* You should have seen the spiteful look in his eyes when he saw you, my baby-child. He just hissed and mumbled something about the house filling up with rats. Rats! That's what your father called you when you were born. And then he named you *Akajun-wa—The hand never rejects a child.*

SHAKARA: *(Angry.)* I said it before. Nobody wants me now. Nobody wanted me before. Nobody cares. And you now want me to listen? Is it fair? Look Mama! Think! Is it fair?

KECHI: *(Rising.)* Are you being fair to her, yourself? *(Height-*

ened tension. OMESIETE pulls KECHI to the side and motions to her to go inside. KECHI leaves, leaving mother and daughter alone.)

OMESIETE: *(Calmly.)* Now child, tell me what I need to know. Ever since the school break, you have changed a lot. You've been angry. Restless. Impatient.

SHAKARA: Haven't I always been?

OMESIETE: But never like this. Am I not your mother? As a mother should, I watch my children. Look into their eyes, listen to their voices to see just where they are at all times. It's my duty. And I'm doing the best I can, if only you'd let me. Otherwise, how can I help you if I don't know you or your needs?

SHAKARA: It's no use trying if you've already done your best.

OMESIETE: But then help me to continue. To succeed. Try! Try! Try! That is my song. The anthem that I've learnt from life.

SHAKARA: Why is it that some people don't even try at all, or maybe just a little, and they get all they want? Eh, Mama! Don't you see?

OMESIETE: Child, I know what you mean. But...

SHAKARA: *(Charged.)* But what? What Mama? I'm tired of hearing but-but-but! How can anyone go through life like this? Why should I be so young and so ashamed of myself? Yes, I am! And for good reasons too. When am I ever going to have the chance to live like my mates? Eh? Do you know how often I get taunted by other kids about my old worn out second-hand clothes?

OMESIETE: Does it matter? My dear, you're not what you wear.

SHAKARA: But what? *(Sobbing.)* What am I? Who am I?

OMESIETE: Oh, poor Baby. If only you'd learn the art of patience and perseverance.

SHAKARA: Mama, I'm tired. Tired of being ridiculed and laughed at by other girls who are not even as pretty as

24

myself. The way they look down on me? My clothes as if I carry shit on my body? Ah! And you should see the teachers. The Principal! Even the Reverend Sisters and Fathers are so partial! They always have their favorites; rich people's children, of course. The rich parents can come in with their long, shiny cars any time, any day, to visit. But the poor parents? Ah, Mama! You should see the Principal chasing them away, like flies. Following the Principal's orders, even the gateman slams the gate in their faces, while he runs to open it for the rich parents with their long, long cars. It's only me, well Kechi too, and other poor children who...have to...to...*(Voice cracking.)* Oh, Mama! Others have everything. But not me. Not me. Why? Why? Why?

OMESIETE: *(Cuddling her.)* Your time too will come, Baby.

SHAKARA: When? When? When I'm old? Forty? Fifty, with everything flabby like...like... *(Indicating her mother's.)* Oh Mother, believe me, I've tried and I'm tired.

OMESIETE: *(Amused.)* Ha! Already? Just how long have you been trying?

SHAKARA: For seventeen whole years! That's a lifetime!

OMESIETE: *(Loud laughter.)* Oh, dear! Seventeen? A lifetime? Child, you amuse me. I'm past forty and I'm still trying. *(Takes up the girl's hand and, side by side, they start walking towards the audience.)* Ah, life's journey! A long road. A very long, long road that is sometimes straight. Many crooked. And bumpy. What else can I say? Child, you've only just begun. On this journey you must arm yourself with these time-released vitamins: *Patience! Perseverance! And Prudence!* Don't you ever give up! Nobody gets anywhere by giving up.

SHAKARA: I've seen the way things get turned around mere. Even the law gets turned around to suit some people. The rich and powerful ones. Is it fair?

OMESIETE: What is fair? How do you measure fairness?

SHAKARA: With justice.

OMESIETE: From whose eyes? Ah, child! In time, you, too,

will learn the art of justice. Justice wears many faces. It's not always fair. Same thing with life.

SHAKARA: Mama, it hurts. Think about it. You mothers who don't listen to your children! Listen! Think about what your children say and feel too. Mother, children have their pains and stories too!

OMESIETE: My daughter, I understand. Perfectly. Children, and even adults, can be wicked to one another in such a way that it hurts and pricks right into the bone marrow. Taunting and ridiculing? Not new to me either. I, too, have been there. When I was married to your father, I could never afford the latest fashions in lace, velvet, and silk that other women displayed in churches and meetings. That is why you must stay in school to arm yourself with education because, that is the power you need for tomorrow. *(Pause.)* That is why you cannot afford to drop out of school. Because it will be too expensive for you. For us. For the future. You already know where I'm coming from. We need to break this cycle of failure and poverty that's crippling us. That is the only way out. Forward!

SHAKARA: There is nothing anybody can do or say to make me go back to that stuffy place. See the graduates out there? Any jobs for them? So don't force...

OMESIETE: Oh no. Nobody can force you to do what you don't want. The best I can do as a parent is to help you see where you're headed. I can only give you my own insights to help guide you through the long, tedious roads along life's journeys.

SHAKARA: Don't worry. I know just where I'm going. I can see it.

OMESIETE: But I can't.

SHAKARA: Then rest yourself. I'll be just find. And you'll be much happier in the end.

OMESIETE: Even when you fall?

SHAKARA: That too is fine. I'll get back on my feet again.

26

OMESIETE: Well, child. You have youth smiling now on your side. Don't waste it. And who knows? Maybe you're right. But who can tell tomorrow? I'm not God to see that far. I may be your mother, but I'm not your God, and can never be. We all have our paths. So if you have chosen, then it's up to you. I cannot change anyone's path of destiny.

SHAKARA: Mama, it's not been fair.

OMESIETE: Child, I hear you. But one should still make the best of it. Every situation. No matter how bad. See the brighter side.

SHAKARA: Mama, I'm just tired. Tired of looking so hard and seeing nothing. Tired of being trampled upon...as if...

OMESIETE: That shouldn't bother you. Believe...in yourself. With hard work, with your education. Someday...you too will become...

SHAKARA: *(Rising.)* I want to be *now!* I want to be that *Somebody,* now!

OMESIETE: Babe, you cannot force the sunrise!

SHAKARA: You can, if you must.

OMESIETE: Can you force the milk-teeth? Ask anybody!

SHAKARA: I don't have to ask anybody. I know it for myself.

OMESIETE: Aha! Tell me what you know child that your mother doesn't know. *(SHAKARA breaks into a smile.)* Yes, we're poor. Say it. But don't be ashamed of who you are. We're not the only poor people in the world. Carry yourself with respect and dignity. Then tell those who laugh at you that *Life is like a river. It flows. No condition is permanent, after all.*

SHAKARA: But ours is. Why us? Why must we be different?

OMESIETE: Because we are. Everybody can't be the same. Is the leopard the same as the lion?

SHAKARA: But they look alike. And they both can boast of

their sharp claws.

OMESIETE: Babe, I know. But still, the leopard has its spots. Tell those who laugh at you that even without being a lion, like a leopard, you too are proud. Proud of your own paws and spots.

SHAKARA: *(Violently.)* Damn those spots, Mama! I'm tired and fed up with spots and spots. Why? Why should it be me? Always me...us? You, too, listen to me Mama. I don't want no spots. No more. No! All I want is my fair share. To be just like others. Just like other girls my age. That's all.

OMESIETE: *(Smiling, caressing her hair.)* My dear, I understand. But you can't rush life. We must work hard and take our turn. As I said, a leopard is a leopard; not a lion. A chicken can only be a chicken, not an eagle.

SHAKARA: *(Bragging.)* Mama, I want to be that eagle. Not a chicken!

OMESIETE: I know. Don't we all? Follow your dreams, child. Fly high, but mind you don't get burnt. There is to much heat on the road out there, we do not know.

SHAKARA: Then leave me alone to find out for myself.

OMESIETE: Am I holding you? You're free. Free to fly. *(Pause.)* Only beware of the stormy weather ahead.

SHAKARA: Let it be on me. I know my way. I am the sole author of my life. I won't let you or anybody else direct it for me. So let everyone leave me alone! *(She storms out to the other side and takes her place on her tree stump.)*

OMESIETE: *(Sighing.)* Ah ya-yah! I tried. One can only try. *(Resignedly.)* Child, I've done my duty. The world hears me now. Let whoever says I haven't come, and tell me just what it is I need to now!

KECHI: *(Stepping to the door.)* Mother, you've spoken. No one can say you haven't. But that daughter of yours? Husai! She's stone deaf. Don't kill yourself.

OMESIETE: But what can I do? How can I watch my precious

one go to waste?

KECHI: I know she's your child. But it's up to you. You go on and waste your little energy. I can't afford it. I don't care anymore! *(Annoyed, KECHI goes inside.)*

SHAKARA: *(Back in her spot.)* Don't care! I know nobody cares! So why should I stay?

OMESIETE: Hush your mouth, child! Who says I don't want... don't care?

SHAKARA: No you don't. You have me because you think I'm the cause of your failure.

OMESIETE: *(Hysterical.)* How can any woman blame any child for her failure? How? No child. You're getting it all wrong. You know I want you and do care. Why do you think I named you Nwa-ebu-ni? Precisely that. I believe in children! Children can and do uplift their parents.

SHAKARA: So that's the price children have to pay for being born? Trophies? Ehn? You hold them hostage, to bear your...Well, if that is what you parents want, then you too have got it all wrong. I can't...live for anyone but myself. People must have to carry their own crosses.

OMESIETE: Who has asked you to carry *their* crosses?

SHAKARA: You!

OMESIETE: Me? Never! All I'm asking is for you...for us all to pull together. Work as one strong unit. That's what it means to be family. To make the difference in each other's lives. Look child, if not for me, do it for yourself. I know now, you're young. You see so much life ahead of you. You know I too was once young and saw it so far away as you do now. But I tell you, *She who has cooked longer can boast of more broken pots!*

SHAKARA: Yours is broken. Mine's still in the making. It's my business, not yours!

OMESIETE: *(Incensed.)* Shut that rotten mouth, you insolent child! That is why you'll continue to drift the way you are already. You think it's life? Crawling from one nightclub to another every day?

SHAKARA: Sure!

OMESIETE: Then go wherever you please. But one day, you, too, will remember who I am. May I live to see that day. *(Wailing.)* God! Where are you? Why have you forsaken me? *(Sobbing, she wanders off to the street. KECHI rushes from behind to confront her sister.)*

KECHI: Now you see what you have done, making her weep?

SHAKARA: Shut up, you!

KECHI: Me? Your senior to shut up? You must be crazy. Or you're on drugs.

SHAKARA: So what? Drugged or crazy, it's my head. Not yours. And it's none of your damned business! So shut your mouth. After all, you're the cause of all this.

KECHI: Indeed!

SHAKARA: Of course you are! With your goodie-goodie-ice-cream manners! Get a life, you old maid! *(SHAKARA takes off a scarf, ties it like an old nun and starts mocking KECHI who is now busy sweeping the yard.)*

KECHI: Go behind me, Satan! *(She sings a hymn.)*

SHAKARA: *(Taunting.)* Yes, Holy of Holies! The virgin in a maternity ward. Yeah! *(Changes to a popular tune.)* "Show me a virgin. In a maternity ward..."

KECHI: *(Sing-song.)* Satan you're the loser-o! Satan you're the loser! Jesus is the winner! And I am a winner in the Lord!

SHAKARA: *(Mocking KECHI.)* You Santa-Santa, married to Jesus. Won't you go find yourself a man? And tell your mama, too, to find herself a man. Maybe with that, she'd leave me alone. I'm not the cause of anyone's *wahala*.

KECHI: You're the scourge of this family. You school dropout!

SHAKARA: As if you're better off yourself. *(Mocking.)* Bible study-bible study. Ha! Let me hear! You want me to

30

tell? Everyday, I'm going to church with Brother Gabriel. *(Giggling.)* Holy Whore! One day, we'll all be here to see the baby Gabriel born. Right here in this God-forsaken slum. Then we'll truly be blessed with a ghetto angel. Ha!

KECHI: *(Kneeling down to pray.)* Father, forgive them for they know *not* what they do.

SHAKARA: Who says?

KECHI: I say! The Lord has spoken through me.

SHAKARA: *(Parodying her.)* I shay! *(Spitting.)* T'fia kwa. Everyday, the Santa-Santa, Kechi, The Great Princess of the Slum runs to this church and that. *(Speaking in tongues and chanting.) I'm Born Again-I'm Born Again!* What is Her Holiness searching for? Salvation! Her Holiness says she's looking for the way. Her Way is buried in the Church. Hey?

KECHI: At least, mine's better. I'm looking for salvation. But you? What do you do? Pros...sl... *(She goes into a mock chant.)*

SHAKARA: *(Mocking.)* "Armageddon! Repent! The end is near. Jesus is coming. Come, you all! Repent and be saved! I'm saved! Ha! Ha! Ha! Oh, yes. I hear you. Indeed, Her Holiness is saved in hell. A golden stool's reserved for her in this hell of a home. Ha! *(Stops suddenly. Bursts into a hysterical laughter then chants: "Allelu? Alleluhia! I say Allelu? Alleluiyaa! Allelu! Jeeeeeeeee! Jehova! Jesus! Jesus is coming. Coming-Coming-Coming-Jeee-Jesu-Jeee-zus!")*

KECHI: Don't you dare play with my Lord! Satan! Away with you! Out of my sight you *Born-Again Pagan! (KECHI pulls a piece of firewood from the pile and aims it at her sister.)*

SHAKARA: Just try. Try me, you *Born-Again-Nothing.* I say try! *(KECHI strikes her and the girls break into a fight. Attracted by the commotion, the CITY HOODLUMS return and keep urging the girls to fight. The girls lock horns.)*

31

SHOW BOY ONE: Me I no go gree! I no gree if na me. Slap me? And I no break him head? Wetin? And stick dey for my hand? *(An alarmed OMESIETE rushes in to pull them apart.)*

OMESIETE: See what you are doing to yourselves? If you have no shame, I have.

SHAKARA: *(Panting.)* Just tell your daughter to leave me alone.

KECHI: *(Jumping at her.)* You too, leave me!

OMESIETE: Stoooooooop!

SHOW BOY ONE: No lef-am!

SHOW BOY TWO: Hollam!

SHOW BOY ONE: Catch-am!

OMESIETE: Go away, you idlers! Leave my pickin!

SHOW BOY TWO: *(Teasing.)* I touch am?

OMESIETE: Busybody, go away before I pour this mud water on you. You think I will let any of my daughters end up with a thing like you? People go forward, not backward. We have enough worries. Go find yourself other victims. Out! You good-for-nothing touts! *(They resist. OMESIETE gets a scoop of muddy water and sprays it on the HOODLUMS. Meanwhile, the fighting intensifies. The girls' shouts linger in the background even when the hoodlums have disappeared.)* Now you two, stop! Stop, I say! Won't you hear me? Why do you want to make me a laughing stock, ehn? Are we the only poor people in this place? Stop, Kechi!

KECHI: No Mama. This doesn't concern you. It's either me or her today. Or we'll both die.

SHAKARA: Me to die with a wretch like you? No way! *(KECHI aims again with the stick.)*

OMESIETE: That's my firewood you're about to waste for nothing. *(OMESIETE snatches the piece of firewood.)* Now go on and fight. Fight and kill yourselves. But not with my firewood. No! I paid dearly for it. For everything in all my life. Now, go on and kill each other just because...we're...(Wailing.) Stop! Have pity on me. Help! Is there no one to help a tired woman? I have no peace. I have no home. (Brandishing a piece of paper.) Look, the Madam just served me her quit notice.

SHOW BOY ONE & TWO: (Returning.) You no fit do am alone again?

OMESIETE: No! Help me somebody!

SHOW BOY ONE & TWO: Women with dem big, big mouth like fish wey commot for water. (Teasing.) "Help ! Help Meeee! (The HOODLUMS laugh and break up the fight.)

OMESIETE: Thank you. But please leave us alone. (Still giggling and teasing, the HOODLUMS depart. OMESIETE pulls KECHI to the coconut tree.) Come with me. (To SHAKARA.) You deaf one. If I were you, I'd go buy me a good pair of ears. Or better still, another mother!

SHAKARA: You think you have to tell me? You watch! I'm on my way and it won't be long now.

OMESIETE: Do I blame you? It's my fault. It's children like you who make a woman re...gre...

SHAKARA: And you think I don't? I regret every day of my life. (Turns away.)

OMESIETE: (Throwing yams to her.) For once, Miss-Do-Nothing. Go make yourself useful. Do something and stop talking rot. At least, if you can't help with anything else, cook. Cook something for us to eat. And God knows we're starving in this house! It's such a long day and nobody has eaten yet. And with the landlady threatening me to pay the rent? Where do I go? What am I going to do? I'll go to beg her now for more time. That's all I can do. God knows I'm trying my best. (Departing.) I'll soon be back. If you both like, kill each other in my absence. I'm tired! Tired and fed up! Sometimes, I just wish I could end it all. God, where are you? Take me! Take this wretched life away! Ah ya-ya-yah! (SHAKARA bursts into laughter. OMESIETE is so incensed, she lifts a broken piece of wood and aims it at SHAKARA, but she escapes to the other side. Frustrated, OMESIETE con-

fronts her rude daughter. But KECHI is already stand-
ing between them; pleading. Suddenly, sounds of "The
Beast" screeching to a halt. The car engine runs as the
driver quickly opens the door and stands at attention
while the pompous CHIEF CHAIRMAN escorts the glam-
orous MADAM KOFO out the door with a parting kiss.
The landlady struts into OMESIETE's yard.)

THE THIRD STAGE

The Cobra in Her Nest

(Shocked, OMESIETE and her daughters freeze. They soon recover and greet MADAM KOFO who's adorned in gold and other expensive jewels. OMESIETE motions to her daughters to go inside. The two women stand face-to-face. Silence.)

MADAM KOFO: *(Strutting.)* Well, Missis-what-do-you-call yourself? *(Pause.)* I wouldn't be that harsh on the child if I were you. After all, she's not the cause of your misfortune, is she? *(OMESIETE still staring at her boss.)* Yes, Ma'am! "Mississi!" That girl is not one of the pests eating up my precious weeds, is she? If I were you, I'd get more serious with the job. Tending every seed in that farm like my newest-born child. You hear me? *(Silence.)* Or be ready to move out, now! You hear me? *(Silence.)* You understand? I'm disappointed, very disappointed. I appointed you head-farmer because you were jobless. I employed you for your past record....I mean your nanny service....caring for my daughter. *(Pause.)* But see now how ungrateful you have become. Ruining my business. And...trying to take my child away from me.

OMESIETE: *(Stunned.)* Me? Who? What? Ma...?

MADAM KOFO: Stop right there! Don't "Ma" me. I'm not older than you. Am I? *(Silence.)* So stop acting so...so... I've been wandering...looking all over the place for my daughter. Until I found her here.

OMESIETE: I was working in your plantation, and you know how far that is. So how am I to know that you've been looking for your daughter?

MADAM KOFO: As if that's news to you.

OMESIETE: What? Dupe missing?

MADAM KOFO: Stop acting so innocent. Didn't I see her in this place a moment ago? Don't play tricks on me now. I told you, I don't want my daughter anywhere near your lot!

OMESIETE: What is my business with your daughter?

MADAM KOFO: You tell me. *(Silence.)* Something tells me that you people are trying to use my daughter against me. Is Dupe not always running to you? Just the other day, my own child boasted that you're the...only mother she's ever known. Whoever heard that?

OMESIETE: And is that my offense? What's my business if you have an argument with your daughter? What business has the fish with a raincoat?

MADAM KOFO: A lot. To take her...what belongs to me? You think I'll live to see you do that? Over my dead body! And make sure you get your useless daughter with her long wayward legs to stay away from my daughter. A death trap you all. Sick! My spirit tells me...

OMESIETE: *(Dignified.)* Then tell your spirit to go elsewhere and look for what is making it sick. Certainly not me or my daughter.

MADAM KOFO: You will fail, you all who seek my downfall. I am strong and so is my daughter.

OMESIETE: Then why worry? You have it all.

MADAM KOFO: *(Bragging.)* Dupe knows herself. She'll never allow herself to be influenced by anybody. Not just anybody! Certainly not under my own roof.

OMESIETE: Congratulations! Failure is an orphan, I know.

MADAM KOFO: You've already failed in your schemes to kill my business. Now you're also plotting to put a spell on my only child?

OMESIETE: A spell? *(Raucous laughter.)* I wish I could put that spell on my own daughter! *(Seriously.)* From now on Madam, I beg you please, hold your daughter.

MADAM KOFO: Who are you to tell me what to do with my own child? Nonsense!

OMESIETE: Just keep her with you. I don't want any trouble. *(Pause.)* I know Dupe's very fond of us. But if that is a problem, please keep her in your mansion.

MADAM KOFO: You're jealous. That's all. Did I or anyone tie you down? Is it my fault that...

OMESIETE: That I'm a nobody? Say it. I may be a nobody to you now. But some... somebody....You never know. You're not my creator. *God works in mysterious ways.*

MADAM KOFO: Your business, you charlatan. I know now all your schemes against me. But beware.

OMESIETE: Of what? Did I steal or kill?

MADAM KOFO: You think I'm sleeping? Beware! My eyes are wide open. Take note! Any day I hear anything about my business outside, you alone will have to answer for it.

OMESIETE: *(Protesting.)* Oh, no! Don't put your load on my head. No! I'm carrying enough already. It's unjust.

MADAM KOFO: Who talks about justice?

OMESIETE: I. The world...free to talk...

MADAM KOFO: *(Laughing.)* Ha! Who says you're not free? I appointed you Chief...

OMESIETE: *(Dignified.)* Yes, a head laborer in your plantation. But not *your slave.*

MADAM KOFO: It's your business to keep the secret...keep them quiet. That's why I pay you. Not so?

OMESIETE: So now you pay me to shut people up? Am I the police?

MADAM KOFO: Take it or leave it. Tend my precious seeds.

OMESIETE: Weeds!

MADAM KOFO: *(Vehemently.)* Seeds! Your duty is to kill insects and keep them quiet. Is that too much to ask for keeping a roof over your head with a full stomach?

OMESIETE: Half-empty, Madam.

MADAM KOFO: *(Scornfully.)* Ungrateful wretch!

37

OMESIETE: Call me whatever. I know who I am.

MADAM KOFO: Then add this to your nametag! "Silence." *(Pause.)* Your responsibility is to keep your mouth shut and keep the workers silent at all times. Or else, get ready to pack. And lose the job too. You hear me? *(Silence.)*

OMESIETE: Do I have a voice?

MADAM KOFO: I didn't take yours. So don't take what belongs to me. *(Pause.)* As for my precious seeds which the insects have already eaten, your salary for this month will be used to pay back the loss. And that's final!

OMESIETE: What? My salary?

MADAM KOFO: Do I speak with water in my mouth? You heard me.

OMESIETE: *(Trembling.)* Ye...ye...yes, Ma...

MADAM KOFO: *(Smiling.)* Alright! I thought you did.

OMESIETE: *(Sighing.)* "God dey!" That's a poor wo-man's prayer."

MADAM KOFO: *(Still smiling.)* Does it concern me? Ha! Ha! Ha! *(Exit MADAM KOFO. Again, on the screen, "The Beast" is seen cruising into the premises. OMESIETE stares tearfully at the fragments surrounding her. SHAKARA re-emerges, briefly resumes her adornment over the stump and then goes inside. Lights dim.)*

THE FOURTH STAGE

Love's Labor

(OMESIETE hums a familiar tune as she hoists the label: "Cheap Wood For Sale." KECHI returns and stands staring at her moody. KECHI pulls her along with a bench to the coconut tree. Both of mother and daughter settle down beneath the coconut tree to start cutting up more yam chips.)

KECHI: Mother, we're making progress. *(Lifting the bag of chips.)* See? A whole lot of chips to sell tomorrow.

OMESIETE: But what is it worth?

KECHI: Something, Mother.

OMESIETE: I know. Even a penny counts. *(Silence.)* That woman has changed.

KECHI: How?

OMESIETE: A lot. She used to be much nicer.

KECHI: Really?

OMESIETE: Yes, my dear.

KECHI: That's news to me. I've told you mother, leave that woman to choke on her weeds. Find another job.

OMESIETE: Where? With so many people on the streets? Even graduates are begging for meaningless jobs. Where are the jobs? Where do I go? Without education? Without connections? And without a name?

KECHI: God will provide.

OMESIETE: Well, God better be fast! Because I can't wait anymore. I've been going and going. My breath's running out. And patience? *(Sighs.)*

KECHI: Everything is in short supply.

OMESIETE: Except pain. Hate. And meanness. Ah! How money transforms people! A-ya-ya-yah! Money. I've become irrelevant to her, and so has everyone else. Since she found this new love: her precious weeds, or nursery, as she calls it.

KECHI: Does she ever find time for her daughter? No. It's just money-money-money and her deadly business! That woman makes me sick.

OMESIETE: She makes everyone sick. *(Sighs.)* Ever since "she made it," her millions as she boasts, she's been finding fault with me and all the other poor laborers. She fired the old cook who's served her for years, just like that. Now it's my turn. Ah, Life! *(Sighs.)* I've been on this thorny, rocky road before; like when your father abandoned me. As they say, *Dead body no be new thin for ground. (Smiles.)* You know, I used to work with the daily-paid laborers who carried cement for a construction company? Then, five years ago, the Madam came to me. Complained bitterly that her laborers were reckless and ripping her off. She needed an old, reliable hand to nurse her precious weeds. If I agreed to come back, she promised to make me the Chief Laborer.

KECHI: So insulting! Why didn't you reject it?

OMESIETE: *(Laughing.)* Child, how could I? You reject an offer when you have a better option.

KECHI: But what's the difference? You were already trapped in labor.

OMESIETE: Child, you do not understand. I'm getting on in years, you know. How can I live the rest of my life carrying heavy bags of cement? Huh! My bones are getting weak. They need rest.

KECHI: But you're still in labor...I mean you're laboring.

OMESIETE: I know. But this is different. I'm no longer a daily-paid laborer. It's more stable. Then I have this small place to rest my aching bones. Don't you know we'll be paying more or remain homeless if we didn't have this place? It's more dangerous out there, you know.

KECHI: We're stuck.

OMESIETE: Be positive. My God is not sleeping. Neither are my ancestors. They didn't bring me to this world to suffer forever. *(Smiling.) Onye-ma-echi?* Who knows tomorrow?

KECHI: Your landlady...She thinks she's God.

OMESIETE: Nobody is God. She might have power over me but God...*(Sighs.)* How wealth changes people! And she's wise.

KECHI: Street wise.

OMESIETE: Whatever. But it's at least leading her far.

KECHI: To Hell! Didn't you take care of her child?

OMESIETE: *(Gentle admonition.)* Sh...Ke-chi!

KECHI: Ma! That woman has forgotten. But her child still remembers. Isn't it why Dupe's always here running to us? Now the mother turns around and blames everybody else.

OMESIETE: But herself! Ha! The rich and powerful ones! Who would have told me that a woman like me would turn out to be the thorn in my flesh?

KECHI: Now you know, Mother. But she has no power over you. Only her bottom power! *Ikebe Super!* Let her go and die!

OMESIETE: Hush your mouth, child! How can you abuse an adult like that? Respect your elders!

KECHI: If an adult respects me, I respect...

OMESIETE: Ohoooo! You too? You're beginning to sound like your sister. Is one wild cat not enough? Child, I've had it. And you better be careful!

KECHI: Mama, it's not me. All of us get our reward for whatever we do. That woman will be paid back in her own coins.

OMESIETE: Nobody is God. Only God knows what tomorrow will bring.

KECHI: You'll see. Vultures will lick her eyes.

OMESIETE: *(Scolding.)* Kechi! Are you crazy? You're not usu-

41

ally rude to your elders. What's come over you?

KECHI: That should tell you something, Mother. Better start preparing to move...for the landlady's obituary. I see it coming. *(Jubilantly.)* "Obito!" for the thick Madam! "The bigger they are, the harder they fall"!

OMESIETE: *(Reciting.) Thou shalt not kill.* Remember?

KECHI: But soldiers do. The government pays them to commit...

OMESIETE: Child, shut your mouth! I can see you really want to put me in trouble. *(Pause.)* You've forgotten that we still live in her house and that I still have to work for her? If she dies, where are we going?

KECHI: Mama, don't you worry. Didn't the bible say, "Look at the ravens. They have no barns and yet daily, they do find food to eat. And the lilies? Even King Solomon in all his glory wasn't more beautifully clothed. So if the birds and the lilies of the earth can, how much more you, beloved and trusting in the Lord?

OMESIETE: True. My hands are clean. *(Sighing.)* Ah, life! Life's like a river. It flows. Everything takes its course. Nobody gives or controls life.

KECHI: Except the Almighty, I know. But leave her. God will take care. *(Chanting.)* "Revenge not, for vengeance is mine," says the Lord.

OMESIETE: Leave everything in God's hands. I know we cannot question God. But sometimes I wonder why God sits patiently while those who have, get more. And those who don't, lose even the little that they have. With us poor, we keep losing and losing. It's so hard to come up when you're down already.

KECHI: So give up? Keep trying!

OMESIETE: Hard luck. Life's problems are like chicken shit. Sometimes you scrub and scrub to wipe it off. But even then it sticks; makes your muscles tight. Sometimes they get so tight you can't even move forward or backward. All you can do is stay. Waiting for time to blow it away. Slowly. Gently. We learn to forget. Time, the ultimate teacher and healer leading us to forget. The eternal balm that heals all wounds! As no one can tell the true face of God, none too can tell the true face of time. This is what my mother used to say. *(She starts packing her wood inside.)*

KECHI: *(Lifting a bundle.)* They say, "When it rains, it pours."

OMESIETE: My dear, it's been raining here for a very long time!

KECHI: *(Chuckling.)* Mother, for as long as I can remember!

OMESIETE: Believe. Have faith. Work hard. Pray. May God's will be done.

KECHI: *(Loudly.)* Amen! *(OMESIETE breaks into a song. KECHI joins her.)*

OMESIETE: *I have to go and beg her.*

KECHI: That devil?

OMESIETE: Hush. It is not everything a palm-wine tapper sees on the tree top that he talks about.

KECHI: I know Mother. But...

OMESIETE: No 'but' anything. Humility pays. If I say to her 'please' or 'sorry', that won't remove one single hair from my body. It doesn't make me less of who I am or what I am. But it does assure me a roof over my head.

KECHI: You don't have to crawl and beg her as if she's God.

OMESIETE: Remember what I say to you always? "It's the hand which receives that needs to stretch longer."

KECHI: I hear you.

OMESIETE: Keep working. I'll soon be back. *(OMESIETE heads for MADAM KOFO's estate. Lights dim. KECHI intensifies her labor on the chips as she sings the blues. With head hanging down, SHAKARA crosses over and approaches her sister.)*

SHAKARA: See? It's all your fault.

KECHI: Yours!

SHAKARA: Yours!

KECHI: She wouldn't be so terrified if not for you.

SHAKARA: Liar! It's because of you she's always...

KECHI: What?

SHAKARA: Comparing.

KECHI: You expect her not to? Mother may be poor but you think she's an idiot, ehn? You think she's so wretched that she can't tell when she's being violated? And by her own, eh? Just know this: Whatever she is, she's my mother. And I'll stay by her to the glorious end. She's my mother.

SHAKARA: She's my mother too!

KECHI: *(Sarcastically.)* Shiooooo! So you know? Tell me, so she's your Mama? That's news to me. I didn't know that you knew where you came from.

SHAKARA: Does it concern you?

KECHI: It does because she is my mother. So don't kill her for me!

SHAKARA: And she's my mother too!

KECHI: At least, one thing in life that we both agree on.

SHAKARA: *(Mocking and applauding.)* Congratulations! *(Uneasy silence.)*

KECHI: Whatever your reason, I find it extremely difficult to understand why you hate your own mother.

SHAKARA: Who says I hate her? Nobody but you, "Tatafo." Gossip! And just get this into your fat bloody head. I don't hate her. *(Tearfully.)* I'm just only ashamed of...

KECHI: Ashamed of your own mother? *(Parodying.)* 'I don't hate her. I'm just only ashamed of...!' Go on, say it! Sha-ka-ra, Dance-Hall Queen! 'I don't hate her. I'm just ashamed...' Nonsense! Cut off your wide "W" nose then. Is that why you're always bleaching and scrubbing your skin? You self-hater! Go buy yourself some love!

SHAKARA: *(Tearfully.)* You too. You're just pretending. Like

44

me, you too would want to be like Dupe, and other rich people. Don't you wish we had their wealth? Aren't you jealous of their fortune?

KECHI: Of course. Like everyone, I too would like to have the money and privilege to make life easier. But, I tell you, I won't go for it at all costs. We're struggling, alright. But everything in life takes time and patience. And I will never sell myself and good name for money!

SHAKARA: *(Loud laughter.)* Yeah right! Saint Kechi!

KECHI: Mock me for all I care. You can't change me. I am me. And you are you. No matter who one becomes, home is home. Without it, one is rootless, and can wither.

SHAKARA: Hey *Preacher*, I hear you! Just go on with your sermon. And you know what? You can't change me either. I've said it and say it again. If you're not ashamed of this stinking hole we're in, I am. Just a little while and I'm out of here!

KECHI: Shame on you if you don't leave.

SHAKARA: You wait and see!

KECHI: Go on and hate yourself. It's your right. I'm tired of people going about hissing and sulking around the house as if...Well, I don't know. *(Pause.)* Is it a crime to be poor?

SHAKARA: *(Emphatically.)* Yeees! Poverty is a crime!

KECHI: *(Mock laughter.)* Hnm...I see. So it is now a crime to be poor? Whoever heard that before?

SHAKARA: Now you know.

KECHI: *(Abandons the chips and starts piling up the wood for sale as she speaks.)* Poverty. So that is why you despise your own family? Eh? Well, I'm learning, everyday.

SHAKARA: Why shouldn't I? Is it not the same country we live in with Dupe, her mother and their neighbor? That Uncle Shanka? Don't you see where they live?

KECHI: Where?

SHAKARA: Paradise. No problem whatsoever. *(Holding her sister, and pleading passionately.)* Dupe. You should see

45

Dupe's room. And her mother's? Ah!

KECHI: It's their luck.

SHAKARA: Oh stop it! What's luck got to do with it?

KECHI: Well, it does. What else do you want me to say?

SHAKARA: Luck has nothing to do with it. Believe me Kechi. We've got to do something.

KECHI: Like what?

SHAKARA: Like...like...*(Frustrated.)* Oh, I don't know. Anything. But something...Just anything to lift us out of this mess. *(Silence.)* Don't you see how rich others are?

KECHI: And then? Everyone with their own destiny.

SHAKARA: *(Passionately.)* Oh, Kechi! Think! Why should we be the ones to be poor? Why? Why do we have to suffer like this? Think about it Kechi. Think!

KECHI: *(Calmly.)* I certainly understand your own sentiment. But your rage is directed at the wrong people. Some people are paid to rule this country, you know? Why don't you ask them? Target them instead of punishing your family. There are so many families who can't even afford one decent meal in a country as rich as ours. You can't blame Mama. She's not the cause of anything.

SHAKARA: Then who is?

KECHI: You think she won't like to ride in a long car? Adorn her neck with gold trinkets like Madam Kofo? Go on summer vacation abroad like all those thick madams?

SHAKARA: Are we dead? Day in, day out, you strain, hauling sacks of...of...Abi? That's some expensive weed, you know? So what stops Mama from working for herself. Getting her own and hauling her own weed, ehn? Well, that's what I call 'Business.' *(Laughs.)* And look, my "Area Mother." That's what it takes to get ahead.

KECHI: And land in jail? Mama won't do just anything to get rich.

SHAKARA: She's lazy...afraid. That's all.

KECHI: Who, Mother? You're either drunk or you don't know her at all.

SHAKARA: I would do anything if I were her, instead of suffering like this. I would certainly do anything to get ahead. Any reasonable person would do just anything to get there.

KECHI: Where?

SHAKARA: I don't know. Somewhere. Someplace. Go to the affluent areas: Victoria Island, Leki Beach, Ikoyi, Maitama, Asokoro...and...and...Oh, Kechi? Why are you so...so resigned? Let's try to change it. Turn things around for us!

KECHI: Is that why you changed your name to Shakara? I don't see how the name "Shakara" makes you feel richer.

SHAKARA: Well I do. At least, I don't have to explain the meaning to people. All those curious people out there, who're always asking you the meaning of your name? *(Mimicking.)* 'Nwa...Nu-wa...ebu...ni...' How do you say that? What does it mean? I just can't take it anymore. Why should I always be different? I want to be like others. That's all.

KECHI: Stop deceiving yourself. I am older than you and I've seen more Xmas days than you. Learn to be content with what you have. Or try to change it for the better.

SHAKARA: Exactly! That's just what I'm going to...

KECHI: By whitewashing old names and putting up false appearances like that useless wig? I mean, those things make me sick. Today you are blonde. Tomorrow, you fry, you bleach, you curl...For God's sake, what do you think you're doing to yourself?

SHAKARA: Helping myself. In case you don't know, it's my life, not yours. Mind your own business!

KECHI: Self-deceit. We could be better off in our state if we all worked hard enough to change it. But I don't think we'll change our fate for the better without honest hard work. No need loitering around. Or donating our bodies to men who are forever demanding. I mean, let's get it clear. We have to help Mother to help us. Don't you feel sad the way she sweats in Madám Kofo's weed farm? And all the thank you she gets from her is abuse. And with you adding insult to injury? For goodness sake, what do you expect? You think she's a piece of wood?

SHAKARA: *(Takes out a mirror to put on her red lipstick.)* No! Neither am I. I'm going off now. Thank you goodie-goodie. Her Holiness, Reverend Kechi, the Great! Remember, "The destiny of the hen is not the destiny of the cock." Isn't that what Mama says? *(OMESIETE returns with some wrapped food. Her singing voice is heard before she's seen.)*

OMESIETE: Now children, I know it's been a long day. And with empty stomachs? We live by faith. Our God doesn't sleep. Come. *(She starts spreading a mat and unwraps the food package. The girls stay away, eyeing each other.)* Come children, it's getting cold. We've had enough bile to feed on for just one day. Come, Kechi. Ebuni! Mama has something for you. Eat. *(Reluctantly, silently, the girls settle down to eat with their mother.)* Tomorrow is another day. And we must start the labor early. You heard what the landlady said: 'Kill the bugs, or lose your job and place.' I need the help. We're all going to the plantation tomorrow.

KECHI: Yes, Ma.

SHAKARA: Count me out. I won't be there.

KECHI: But why?

SHAKARA: *(Firmly.)* Because I won't be there!

OMESIETE: Where will you be?

SHAKARA: Gone!

KECHI: Then better hurry up.

SHAKARA: Don't worry. I'm on my way.

OMESIETE: To where?

SHAKARA: Do I always have to tell?

KECHI: Of course!

OMESIETE: As long as you're here with me.

SHAKARA: Well, too bad. I'm not.

OMESIETE: *(Softly.) Eneke-Nti Mpko!* Oh, deaf one! Didn't you hear the landlady?

SHAKARA: She wasn't talking to me. Was she?

OMESIETE: Babe, so you're not concerned that we're going to be thrown out of this place if one more weed is eaten up by bugs? Ehn? *(Silence.)* And my salary seized! A woman like me is tormenting me and my own child simply shrugs her shoulders and walks by? Ehn? Don't you know what that means to this family? Huh? Don't you know me anymore? Who would have told me? Ah-ya-ya-ya! Ah, Omesiete! No matter how poor, I cannot forget who I am. My name, my pride. The only royal garment I have. *(Pounding her chest.)* It's me, Ome-sie-te. *Someday, I too will be... I, Omesiete! Daughter of Ejeme! (Chanting about her pedigree.) Daughter of Ato-chi! My father, Diji! Ogbuu ji-wa-aka-nga-na-ba! Hand that tends yams that grow into many branches. Yes, I am! Daughter of Oka-Onwene! My mother...Mother of mothers! Nnem Omenka! Hand that weaves intricate patterns of threads to clothe the world! (Sighing.) Ah, death! You broke my right arm when you took my own away! Onwu-di-njo! Death, you wicked one! Why? (Furiously shaking up SHAKARA.)* Child, if only you knew your value. Your heritage. How could you throw all that away?

SHAKARA: Worthless. What have we got to show for it? Besides, I don't care!

OMESIETE: *(Sitting.)* Then I shouldn't worry anymore. Go wherever you please. But I don't have to kill myself to send you back to school when the holiday is over. You want me to pay your school supplies with my blood?

SHAKARA: *(Loud laughter.)* School stuff? Don't worry. I'm not going back there. It's no use now.

OMESIETE: School, no use? So you mean you're really dropping out of school?

SHAKARA: Yes, I've said it! It has no use for me, at least not now. Go count the graduates. How many of them are out there hunting for jobs? Eh?

OMESIETE: Silly girl. Don't you know my story? Learn from me!

SHAKARA: Exactly what I'm doing. Learning fast!

OMESIETE: What will it pay you to fall by the wayside like I did? *(Silence.)* You'll live to regret it, you know.

SHAKARA: *(Chuckling.)* Then it's all in the family. In any case, your story can't be mine. You are you. And I am me. I got a better plan.

OMESIETE: Than education? *(Wailing.)* Ah, my ancestors! *Ejeme Aniogo!* Do you hear her? Or am I the one who is deaf?

KECHI: Why worry, Mama? She's got her plans. Forget. Let's eat. *(Silences as SHAKARA is washing off her hands. OMESIETE tries to stop her.)*

OMESIETE: *(Sternly to SHAKARA.)* Now hear me for the last time. Whatever you do, get ready for tomorrow.

SHAKARA: *(Defiantly.)* I'm not going!

OMESIETE: I hear you. But take note: tomorrow, we're all going to that plantation to kill the bugs so that her weeds may live.

SHAKARA: *(Laughing.)* Me? In that plantation? Never! Have you and that boss of yours ever heard of the miracle called Insecticide? *(Mock laughter. Then silence.)*

KECHI: *(Breaking the silence.)* So Mama, what did the landlady really say?

OMESIETE: That her word is final. No weed, no salary.

KECHI: I knew it. I knew that woman to be as stubborn as a pig.

SHAKARA: Watch your mouth. Have you no respect?

KECHI: Res-what? Look who's talking! Thank God, at last, you know the meaning of the word, res-pect!

OMESIETE: For once, peace! Let's eat. *(SHAKARA sits to wash her hands again, then rises.)* Won't you eat anymore?

SHAKARA: No, I'm full.

OMESIETE: With what? You've only just started. What's the matter?

SHAKARA: Nothing. I've told you, I can't take it anymore.

OMESIETE: *(Concerned.)* Try a little more. It's very good... delicious *Agidi corn meal.*

SHAKARA: I'm done.

KECHI: Why all the fuss? Get lost if you want to!

SHAKARA: Busybody! My business, not yours! *(SHAKARA gives her sister a glare like a cobra watching its prey. Then she grabs her handbag. OMESIETE blocks her way, snatching the bag from her.)*

OMESIETE: Child, it's too dangerous outside. Where are you going?

SHAKARA: I've told you. I got business. I'm going.

OMESIETE: Now? Can't it wait for tomorrow?

SHAKARA: *(Chuckling.)* I've told you. My business can't wait. But as usual, nobody hears or listens to me. When will you both learn that nothing waits for tomorrow?

OMESIETE: Madam, I hear you. Child, you're searching the road for whatever you think you're missing? Mind you get what you ask for! *(Resigned for now, SHAKARA steps back into the shack, returns with her cosmetic bag and starts assembling her altar/shrine around her favorite stump. Silence. OMESIETE offers some of the corn meal wrap (agidi) as she prays. As usual, KECHI starts speaking in tongues as she prays. Crossing over, OMESIETE puts SHAKARA's hand in her sister's.)* That's what you both need.

SHAKARA: What? Leave me alone!

OMESIETE: Child, I cannot make it alone.

SHAKARA: And it's me who can?

KECHI: Nobody is asking you to do anything. Just help out your mother.

SHAKARA: Thank you, Reverend Sister Kechi. But I tell you, at seventeen, killing bugs for a living is not one of my wildest dreams.

OMESIETE: Then whose is it?

SHAKARA: Certainly not for me. Maybe for her. *(Smiling.)* Take that one—your precious 'handbag.' That's what people do with handbags. Since she's your favorite, take her and leave me alone to find my own. I'm going. *(SHAKARA explodes into wild laughter as she rehearses her new dance-steps until she struts far away. Frustrated, her mother scatters her cosmetic altar around and tries to stop her daughter. But SHAKARA flees and it's only the strap of her handbag that OMESIETE is able to reach. As OMESIETE pulls, the strap breaks in her hand, with her other hand holding on to KECHI. OMESIETE stands there, watching helplessly as her daughter disappears. On the street, the CITY HOODLUMS once again appear to accompany her with their teasing, satirical songs.)*

OMESIETE: *(Still holding on to KECHI.)* Come, my daughter. Leave trouble alone. The death which will kill someone doesn't ring a bell. *(Sighing.)* Ah ya-ya-yah! Night is coming. It's been a bad day. But all is not lost. We're still here. Who knows? *(Wry laughter.)* Maybe tomorrow the sun will shine better. As our mothers used to say, "If night hasn't come, how can anyone condemn the day?" Let's look up. Tomorrow.... *(She shrugs, smiles.)*

KECHI: Mother, rest. Leave her to her fate.

OMESIETE: *(Prolonged silence.)* Oooooooooh! *(With KECHI standing by her side, OMESIETE sits on the stump, staring at the broken strap of SHAKARA's bag, until she starts singing a song. KECHI joins her and begins to massage her mother's shoulders. Lights fade out.)*

THE FIFTH STAGE

Love's Red Eyes

(It's late afternoon. OMESIETE appears quite agitated, looking out anxiously for SHAKARA. Determined to wait, she settles down to cut up a piece of fabric to sew as she sings. For a while, KECHI observes her mother struggling with a blunt pair of scissors and the tough fabric. Then she goes to help her straighten and iron out the creases.)

KECHI: Mother, you're so stressed out. Rest.

OMESIETE: My dear, you know how it is here. Sewing is my way of resting.

KECHI: A tedious way to measure rest. Don't you think?

OMESIETE: Well, maybe. But...*(Straining to thread the needle.)* She's still not back. Who knows?

KECHI: *(Distracting her, rubbing her shoulders.)* So Mother, you really thought that landlady would hear you?

OMESIETE: I thought so. At least, if not for now, for the past.

KECHI: No one can remake the past. Isn't that what you always say?

OMESIETE: My daughter. The world beats me beyond all imagination.

KECHI: Nothing new. She's always been that way. *(Cutting up the fabric.)*

OMESIETE: I know that woman. I was her nanny. Remember?

KECHI: Of course I do! How can I ever forget? *(Sighing.)* Ah, mother! The day that wicked woman plays soccer with our heads and buttocks? Our eyes saw stars!

OMESIETE: True?

KECHI: Nhm. *(Play-acting.)* "You orchins!" she screamed as the koboko whip greeted our buttocks. "How dare you play in my sitting room! Is the Boys' Quarters not enough for you?" Chocking and blinded by tears, I ran into the closet. Then she grabbed me. Dipped the knuckles of her right fingers on sand and aimed right at the centre of my head. Sparks flew off my eyes. I'll never forget that day. Since then, I've kept to myself. Never smelt that woman's house again. But your "*Eneke-nti-mkpo*"? The deaf one. Someday soon, she'll hear.

OMESIETE: Hnm...The world grows ears beside their heads. My daughter hangs them behind like decorations. When you talk to her, everything flies across. Viaaaam! I've told her. Play with Dupe. And you know I feel as if that girl is my own daughter? I nursed that child, you know. But her mother?

KECHI: A snake. You suckled a snake's child.

OMESIETE: So you know? Whatever she did to you, it's your fault. What were you little pimps doing in her nest?

KECHI: Just kids playing.

OMESIETE: *(Teasing.)* Ohooo! Count yourselves lucky that the snake didn't bite off your tiny wayward legs. Why did you run?

KECHI: We had to. The fire in that woman's eyes?

OMESIETE: You should have stayed to relish the snake's kiss.

KECHI: Oh, Mama! Stop!

OMESIETE: *(Laughs.)* Silly girl. Have you no fear? There's a lot to fear in life. I keep telling you.

KECHI: Fear another human being? Is she my God?

OMESIETE: You silly girl! Don't you know that all fingers are not equal? Take heed, my daughter. Life is treacherous. Deep like an ocean. It drowns people even when they think they can swim.

KECHI: But I'm trying.

OMESIETE: We try. Keep trying, poor child. Do you know

that even your own friends can betray you?

KECHI: Friends?

OMESIETE: Yes. Spite you. Bite you like a snake behind your back when you least expect it.

KECHI: Then I'll run. Run a thousand miles away from such friends!

OMESIETE: To where? Where will you run to when your bosom friend knows you inside out? They know where you're coming and going. Child, there is no place to hide in this world today, especially when you have an enemy within.

KECHI: I'll fight. Crush it! *(Stomping on the ground.)* Zogbu-zogbu! Enyimba! Enyi!

OMESIETE: *(Laughing.)* Children and faith! Ha! Someday, you, too, will learn that the worst enemy to fight is the one closest to you; the beloved enemy.

KECHI: But why?

OMESIETE: Ha! Have I ever told you the story of the woman who got a snake as her pet?

KECHI: *(Interested.)* No. Tell me. It's been a very long time since you last told us any folktale. I miss that a lot.

OMESIETE: I know. Ah, Palava! Life's tides, sweeping us here and there. But we keep moving. *(She stretches and yawns. KECHI crosses over, drops the pair of scissors and fetches some oil to massage her mother's aching back and shoulders.)* Ah my dear daughter! That feels so good! Your cotton fingers! They feel like the cool lagoon breeze on a hot, sticky afternoon. Ah! It's been such a long time. So long, I don't remember anymore.

KECHI: Mother, count on me. Always. I feel your pain. And I'm here for you. I'll do whatever I can to take your pain away. You know sometimes, I wish I could take it all myself...take it all away.

OMESIETE: No, child. It's we parents who should suffer... endure...live for our children. Not the other way. You children are the seeds of tomorrow. So how can we burden you with the load of today and yesterday?

KECHI: Maybe we can at least share. You take mine, I take yours.

OMESIETE: *(Chuckling.)* The right hand washes the left; the left hand washes the right. That's the way if should be.

KECHI: I hear you. Now tell me the story of the woman with the pet snake.

OMESIETE: Ohoo! That? I almost forgot. Nowadays, I forget too often. I'm learning to forget. Sometimes, learning to forget is just as important as remembering. Otherwise, what would life be without them both: remembering and forgetting? It's an art that everyone should learn.

KECHI: Okay, mother. Will you tell me the story or not?

OMESIETE: You know I will. To you, Mothers may seem talkative. But with all the running around nowadays, moments like these, for me, are rare. Very rare. That is why you now see me relaxing, relishing it and wishing that it would never end.

KECHI: "The priceless moments," as you say?

OMESIETE: Yes, dear! Storytelling as history. The priceless school! *(She chuckles, clears her throat.)* Now the story. Once upon a time, there was this woman who was so rich she didn't know what else to do with her money. Her neighbors nicknamed her "Money-Miss Road." She had everything: cars, mansions, gold, silver, many pets that were fed fat, even when her servants were dying of starvation. To prove that she was richer, bigger, and more daring than anyone else in the world, "Money-Miss Road" decided to court a snake; an animal that no other would dare to approach, not to talk of having it as a pet. The snake was, of course, surprised that anyone in her right senses would make such an advance. At first, the snake couldn't tell if the offer was being made in good faith, so he hesitated. Reminding the woman over and over again, "But I am a snake." "Oh, no. That doesn't matter!" the rich woman dismissed his

56

gentle warning. To win him over, she offered the snake rich comfort and luxurious items, including having a swimming pool to himself and a whole lamb to eat every day. "I will provide you with gold trinkets to adorn your long, shimmering, stately body," she promised. Finally, the snake yielded to her. She took him. For a while, life seemed beautiful. So beautiful for these unusual partners. Every night "Money-Miss Road" would take the snake and make it coil up in her bosom to warm up and caress her. The snake obliged her and they both relished it. But one night the snake reached beyond her navel and gave her a sharp bite that made her bleed and cry. Alarmed and hurt, she jumped out of bed. Pushed her once loving partner out the door, cursing: "You bit me? After all I have done for you? You ungrateful thing! Traitor!" You know what the snake said to the rich woman? "But I told you, I *am* a snake! Remember? You saw me for what I am: a snake. So what have I done wrong? I know my nature. I cannot be anything other than what I am. One can only be true to oneself. But you people of the world want to change everyone. Everything. How can you turn me away from myself? I cannot...must not. That would be one more unnecessary sacrifice in the name of love. If you love me, take me the way I am. If not, then leave me alone to be who I am. So now, goodbye my one-time love!" With that, the snake wound its way gracefully back to where it belonged; in the forest. The rich woman was so hurt, so sick, so heart-broken. She died.

KECHI: Serves her right! Trying to prove something.

OMESIETE: Everything has a price. We pay, dearly.

KECHI: Tell that to your daughter.

OMESIETE: God knows I've tried and tried but she won't listen. (*Pause.*) After all, who am I? Do I have any power?

KECHI: Yes, you do Mother!

OMESIETE: (*Chuckling.*) Are mothers worth anything?

KECHI: A lot!

OMESIETE: Hnm...maybe some...

KECHI: *(Teasing.)* You Mothers rule the world. *Nneka. Mother is gold supreme.* Isn't that what our people say?

OMESIETE: Hnm...maybe before. Not now. Things are changing so fast. One feels dizzy looking. Ah! Time was when parents had power. Not now.

KECHI: But why? What happened?

OMESIETE: It's you children...the youths that we must ask. Worse still, the leaders who have no solution to anything, except how to load up their pockets. Ah-ya-ya-yah! I tell you, the way I see things coming? Tomorrow's babies will be born with full sets of teeth.

KECHI: *(Loud laughter.)* Oh, Mama! Stop exaggerating!

OMESIETE: That's what I tell all parents. Watch out. Fearful times. "What tomorrow will bring will be pregnant and nursing a child at the same time." Our mothers used to say that. But I didn't know what they meant. Now I know. *(KECHI is still laughing and hugging her mother.)*

KECHI: Then tell that to your daughter who has no fear, even of God. That girl will ruin us. Everybody.

OMESIETE: Who knows? Let's not be too quick to judge.

KECHI: Too quick? But we've been in this mess for a lifetime.

OMESIETE: My dear, what else do you expect me to say? Are you both not my blood? As they say, "It may be one mother that gives birth, but it is not the same God that creates." Ha, destiny! That huge baggage that everyone bears. Each one, her own; to bargain with her Chi... God, the final judge and power. Omesiete has no hand in anything except to guide you through your course. *(Pause.)*

KECHI: But that is wrong. You need to do more.

OMESIETE: Like what? Kill myself for her?

KECHI: Oh, no. God forbid! Not that. But parents must feel stronger. Determined. Just say 'No' to any wayward child. If necessary, give her some hard constructive punishment and look the other way, even when she screams to alarm the neighbors. But no. Some parents are just too soft. The moment their child starts to yell and run her mouth like a loose bowel, quickly, they loosen up and succumb. What parents must learn to do is put their foot down. And firmly too.

OMESIETE: *(Laughing and applauding.)* Don't I know it? Our mothers used to say that you slap an erring child's buttocks with your right hand and pull her back with the left. Parenting today is like carrying a hot burning coal on your palm and at the same time being asked to take things easy and not drop it. Babe, you think it's that easy? It burns. Love burns like fire, you know. And it doesn't matter who makes you burn; your child, your husband, your friend, your lover, your mate, even your employer! You children need to know that. And know too that the eagle sweats. Hidden under its fine, strong plumes, the eagle sweats. So do Mothers. Mothers are just ordinary humans, too. Not super humans. What sets them apart from others though, is their dogged strength and courage to persevere against all odds. Like a reed in the tide, often times, they're forced to bend and sway this way and that way, without breaking. Maybe. But then, comes the strong stormy weather that washes everything from the roots, ashore...*(Deep sigh.)* Ah ya-ya-yah1 Ah, children! Don't you know that love is a two-way traffic? Don't you think you sometimes make it too difficult for parents to love you? Ehn? If only you knew how much mothers would do the best for their children. If only...Or how do you think good mothers would like to bring their own children... their own blood into the deep turbulent sea of the world to abandon them? Ah, children! Do you know what our people say? "Na condition make crayfish bend"! Yes, condition! If we don't seem to meet your expectations, it's not because we lack of will. But...the strings of time that pull us away. Or back from where we'd like to be. Ha! You children must help mothers to love you. You think parenting is easy? What you need to know is that every child is different. What works for one may not work for another. Parenting? It's the school we mothers go to learn from trial and error.

KECHI: You parents amuse me. If it's that hard, why bother?

OMESIETE: Because children are the salt. The very essence and season of our lives.

KECHI: *(Amused.)* So you live for your children? Ha! Ha! Ha! If that's so important, you parents need to quit complaining and start living. Or rather, start a school for parenting!

OMESIETE: *(Explosive laughter.)* A school for parenting? My God! Kechi, you're something else. I mean...Teacher. Yes! We'll appoint you the first teacher to that school. Indeed, Children are the best Teachers of Parents!

KECHI: *(Excitedly.)* So congratulate us, parents! Parents, show gratitude. *(OMESIETE makes a mock bow to KECHI.)*

OMESIETE: Yes, Teacher! *(Loud laughter.)* Teacher Nkechi. Thank-You-Thank-You! *(Turning to the audience.)* Did you all hear that? Listen! The teacher is speaking! *(Another bow, another bout of laughter.)*

KECHI: The world listens, except your daughter!

OMESIETE: *(Sighing.)* Ah, that? One can only push so far. Can anyone force the sunrise?

KECHI: No.

OMESIETE: Ah! Then let it be. Leave your sister to her Chi. We look up. Maybe the sun will rise and shine better tomorrow. Night will soon be here.

KECHI: Yes, even the blind can see.

OMESIETE: *(Stroking KECHI's neck.)* Then let's go to sleep.

KECHI: Yes, Mother.

OMESIETE: But before we go...promise me...

KECHI: What?

60

OMESIETE: About the landlady and her brutal beating. You should have told me then.

KECHI: Oh, Mother! You know we can't tell you everything.

OMESIETE: Well, you should.

KECHI: *(Laughing.)* Which children do you know tell their parents everything? Eh? And especially when they do what they're not supposed to do?

OMESIETE: Well, it's up to you. But you see. I've always told you that it's neither helpful to you nor me. Don't hid things from your parents. They can cost you your very life. But I know you teenagers, especially. You want to be independent. You think you can handle everything. Untie the knotty strings of life all by yourself. Ha!

KECHI: But see, Mother! We can! *(She flexes her muscles.)*

OMESIETE: Until you fall and start yelling. *(Mimics an infant cry.)* Nghaa! Nghaa! Mammmmma!

KECHI: Never again. Don't worry. And it's been such a long time. Moreover, I didn't want to upset you. Knowing you the way I do, you would have confronted her.

OMESIETE: Sure! Nobody toys with my children and gets away with it.

KECHI: Yes, my Lioness!

OMESIETE: We're poor, alright. But we must not allow ourselves to be abused or lose our name and dignity. That's the best that anyone has: a name and dignity. It's the fabric that keeps us all from being naked. Never let anyone take that away from you. You hear me now?

KECHI: I hear you, Mother. As you say, "When that is gone, what else is left?"

OMESIETE: That's why I cry when I see your sister hawking herself like a cheap article. "Poverty or not..."

KECHI & OMESIETE: "Nobody can afford to be a plaything!" *(They laugh. OMESIETE breaks into a song and dance. At first, KECHI admires her mother until she joins her. The fading lights slowly follow them into the shack.)*

THE SIXTH STAGE

Meet Freedom Child!

(MADAM KOFO is in her ornate sitting room. She is rich-
ly dressed. Her long blonde hair wig mounted right in
front of her. She cuddles and kisses her bag of precious
seeds/weeds piled up beside her closet as she discusses
a business deal with some partner on the telephone. A
bottle of whisky sits by her side. On a screen opposite
her, DUPE mimics her in a standing mirror, wearing
one of her mother's outfits. She's mocking her mother's
gestures and poking pins into the life-size picture of her
mother reflected on it.)

MADAM KOFO: *(Drinking.)* Haba, Chairman! Darling,
wetin?...*(Laughs.)* And Director on the other line? Hold
on. Hello, my Da-ma-ging Director! Nze! How business?
Yes, life is sweet. Yes. Ehn...My Precious Seed? Yes,
Chief-Darling! You like the last consignment? A new
breed. Americans love it best. You bet. 100% quality.
My God! The best weed you'll find in the market. Yes!
Allah! Saam-saam! Five million. *Shikena!* Yes, right. That
means my next estate is paid for. Yes. One million already paid up to buy our passage. I'm still looking for
a safe courier. Yes! I'm working on it. Will get one soon.
Very soon. No problem. Safety? Very expensive. You
pay for what you get. The ex-law commissioner? Paid
in full. In our corner! The new commissioner? Tough.
Very tough; harassing our partners. We'll get him too.
Maybe raise the stake...his share to five million dollars.
Then he'll loosen up. You know how uptight they are
when they're new. Overzealous; want to impress the
boss. All those self-righteous police. The ex-commissioner? Still very much in our corner. We need the protection from our friends. Yes. Cash and carry. Already
got his share. Chief Chairman. God bless you! Yes, God

is good! He butters my bread! Shikena. Expect the new baggage soon. Yes, a new courier. And remember: cash only. Yes. Pay to use my agent for the Swiss account. The code word? "Holy Seed." Yes. Thank you. Bless you. I'm on my way now. *(Lights a cigarette, calls.)* Dupe! Dupe! Where are you? Come over here, child! *(Quickly, DUPE pulls off her mother's wig and outfit and runs to answer the call. MADAM KOFO appears to be in a great hurry now as her daughter stands before her.)*

DUPE: I'm not a child anymore.

MADAM KOFO: *(Smiling.)* Come on, Angel. Business's calling. And I have to go.

DUPE: Mother!

MADAM KOFO: *(Hastily kissing her.)* Yes, dear!

DUPE: *(Stammering.)* I need...I want...

MADAM KOFO: *(Pulling her travel bag.)* What do you want, dear? You know I'll get whatever you ask.

DUPE: You...Moth...Fa...Can't I see...my father? We need to talk.

MADAM KOFO: *(Dressing up.)* Oh, dear! Not now. Can't you see I'm in a hurry to go?

DUPE: You say that all the time.

MADAM KOFO: But this is different. A very important business...

DUPE: Or course! Everything else is more important, but...

MADAM KOFO: *(Mounting her blonde wig.)* How can you say that? You know how busy I am.

DUPE: Always. *(Pause.)* Don't you think it's time for me? Mother, I too have my own business with you!

MADAM KOFO: I know, dear. But wait...

DUPE: If others can't, why should I?

MADAM KOFO: Because they're not here...I mean you're here, with me.

DUPE: Are you sure? I'm not.

MADAM KOFO: Hey, come on Sweetie. Don't be so stubborn

now. You've been a good girl. *(Gives her a quick peck.)*

DUPE: And is that why you never listen to me?

MADAM KOFO: I can...I will. But not now. We'll talk later.

DUPE: When it's too late?

MADAM KOFO: I'll soon be back. Believe me. It won't be long. Go to bed, dear. I'll wake you up when I come back. Then we can talk, even far into the night. There'll be nothing, nobody to separate or interrupt us. But I need to go. *(Giving her another quick kiss. DUPE stands there, coldly watching her mother depart.)*

DUPE: *(At the door.)* Sleep, my Angel. I'm coming back to you soon. Bye, Sweetie!

MADAM KOFO: Goodbye, M...other! *(MADAM KOFO majestically steps out to the gate, with flashes of the chauffer-driven "Beast" waiting outside with the CHIEF CHAIRMAN. As soon as DUPE hears "The Beast" hit the tarmac, she feigns smoking like her mother. She reaches into her mother's closet and begins to mock and make-up herself in her mother's regalia: a ready-made head-tie or gele, a glittering red lace buba, a golden pair of shoes with a matching handbag, a huge stuffed sack of illegal drugs, which she mounts on her buttocks as she struts and mimics her mother. Suddenly, someone knocks at the door. Not sure if it's her mother returning, DUPE stomps the cigarette with her foot, and kicks it under the sofa as she hurriedly dismantles her consume. She peeps out and sees SHAKARA.)*

DUPE: *(Excitedly opening the door.)* Hnm...So it's you, fathead? I thought it was somebody...

SHAKARA: *(Erotic swings.)* No, it's not. What's up girl?

DUPE: Nothing. *(Looking her up and down.)* But better take off...

SHAKARA: Oh, my shoes? I'd nearly forgotten. *(Takes off the shoes.)* Okay, here. But...is...is your mother home?

DUPE: *(Hesitating.)* Hell, no! But why do you ask?

SHAKARA: *(Agitated.)* Ehnmm...You know...your...

DUPE: Mother? Don't you worry. She's lost.

SHAKARA: *(Still fidgety.)* Come on...You know I dread...

DUPE: She's dead. Relax!

SHAKARA: Oh, Dupe! Stop your pranks!

DUPE: *(Chuckles.)* Now, I'm serious. She's dead. Died today. I choked her.

SHAKARA: It means you're telling me to get ready to go now. I know you don't want me here.

DUPE: *(Giggling.)* Go, girl. You're free. Fly out. But know that time is running out. Rest-in-Pieces. *(She slaps SHA-KARA's backside.)* You wanna party?

SHAKARA: *(More relaxed.)* And rock-'n-rock. *(They start break-dancing.)* So your mother's gone? That's why you're so dry-eyed like a rat, dropped from the roof-top, eh?

DUPE: What if I tell you now she's in?

SHAKARA: *(Quickly grabs her shoes and runs to the door.)* Is she? God save...!

DUPE: *(Pulling her back.)* Silly girl! I thought you were the best known couple in the world. Ha!

SHAKARA: *(Easing herself into the sofa again.)* Don't worry. We'll surprise you someday.

DUPE: Nothing surprises me nowadays. The long awaited moment is here. You're in. She's out. Gone. Gone for-ever. *(Laughs.)* I'll see to that. For you both, there's no way out. Let's celebrate. *(Together, they sing, "Let's Cel-ebrate.")*

SHAKARA: Hooray! The coups! My coups! I am the new General. And you are my Lieutenant! *(Military com-mand with heavy accent.)* Now Lieutenant, salute your General! *(SHAKARA salutes as they play-act, with the General giving the marching orders.)* Left-Right! Left-Right! Elem-Ai! Ai! Elem! Ai-Ai-Ai! Abo-turn! Salute to the General! *(Instead of saluting the General, the Lieu-tenant rebels and salutes self instead.)* Hooray to the Dance-Hall Queen!

DUPE: You're stripped of your ranks! Saboteur! *(She feigns snatching the other's medallion.)* Now return to base. You bloody civilian! Bloody kwa-mmu-nist!

SHAKARA: No. Once a soldier, always a soldier.

DUPE: Halt! You're stripped of your umblic...Fired!

SHAKARA: Wired! I'm wired!

DUPE: I say fired, zombie! *(The rebellious SHAKARA now trembles in fear.)* Aju-wa-ya! Return to base! *(They sing "I remember when I was a soldier." SHAKARA obeys. A flashback to the dazzling spectacle at the nightclub festival follows. Together once again, they briefly re-enact the seductive dance-steps SHAKARA exhibited the day she won her title of "Dance-Hall Queen."* The terrific Shak! No one sees your break-lights. Ride on girl! Baby Bitch!

SHAKARA: Mother-Bitch! *(Pause.)* Your Mama?

DUPE: Ikebe Super! *(Gyrating.)* Let them come see the way you terrorize those jelly men at the Nasty Girls Club.

SHAKARA: *(Suddenly excited.)* Girlfriend, you won't believe this. You know where I've been since you left me today?

DUPE: No. Tell me.

SHAKARA: Well, as usual, I went to nose...

DUPE: Sniffing around for a good time as usual.

SHAKARA: Yeah. Big time party. High society wedding.

DUPE: *(Giggling.)* Another heart waiting to be broken?

SHAKARA: Well, there was this road block. You know the usual thing with the high society thing?

DUPE: Hnm...Empty the treasury. All roads lead to their bellies. Close down the streets!

SHAKARA: Well, my dear. The party was in full swing. Top musicians playing. *(DUPE is swinging and gyrating with her.)*

DUPE: "Murder in the high seas!" You know that saying?

SHAKARA: *(Excitedly.)* Ogbu Ozu! Murder in the high seas.

66

Kill dead-body! That's the new expression for *OBT – Obtained By Trickery – Mafia!*

DUPE: The 419 junta? I see.

SHAKARA: So, hear now. *(Showing her legs.)* With my 'lege-dez benz'...

DUPE: Yes. Your 'leg-size' limousine.

SHAKARA: I tried desperately to gate-crash into this swinging party! But I just couldn't because security was too tight. Well, I never gave up. I waited. Then this "OBT Mafia" boy came cruising at high altitude in that great shiny machine...

DUPE: "The Beast?"

SHAKARA: Got it! The huge python just spread and laid out right in front of me. Followed with a hissing sound. I smacked my lips, lapped...

DUPE: Can't help your greedy soul, eh?

SHAKARA: You know it. So without looking back, I just glided inside as "The Beast" continued puffing and fuming, enough to suffocate the world around. "The Beast" blasted the entire place with his honking. But with no one there to lift the road block, he got loose, brought out his gun and started shooting into the air. Girl, you should have seen the confusion! The whole world running for cover as "The Beast" stood majestic in the crowd. And you know what? He brought out several boxes and started spraying the damned place with the minted green god...I mean new dollar and pound sterling mints. With all that manna falling from heaven, people fell to the ground, scrambling for whatever they could get. In the struggle, we even tore up a dollar note; one half with me, the other with...who knows? I'm lucky. I know I'm gonna make it.

DUPE: Yeah, sure!

SHAKARA: Girl, you should have seen the world hailing him.

DUPE: You don't mean it?

SHAKARA: An 'eye-witness report.' I saw it with my naked eyes.

DUPE: And you got your share?

SHAKARA: *(In Jamaican Patois.)* "What you expek? Me have to!" And with all that hard labor planned for the night? Girl, me just go dem town. Get me enough to last...

DUPE: A lifetime?

SHAKARA: I wish.

DUPE: That *(h)*idiot. Money Miss-Road!

SHAKARA: "I tell you, me stuffed my bra. Me underwear. Any hole at my disposal." As the music played, I put my best foot forward. My body turned vibrator. And the dude didn't miss a thing.

DUPE: How can? They don't miss anything. Gave a good front!

SHAKARA: I was determined to lick him to death, but the boar was clever.

DUPE: He should be, if he's to succeed in the 419 business.

SHAKARA: I thought I could watch him. Pretend to be sleeping. And then, once he dozed off, quietly cart away, at least, two boxes of that green stuff.

DUPE: Go girl! Money-Maniac!

SHAKARA: I plead guilty! *(Pause.)* But then tragedy. Suddenly, that DPO entered with a huge Alsatian. That beast. I hate him.

DUPE: What has he done? He's only a government dog at work. That's all.

SHAKARA: Well, I hate him. Broke up the party. My party. Worse still, he handcuffed my 'Lord.' Asked his men to haul him into the coughing Black Maria outside.

DUPE: And the party was over.

SHAKARA: That dog killed my party.

DUPE: You're lucky you're not in the nest with him. Supposing as you had planned, he'd taken you home? And then the hour of the Lord came and he got captured? You, too, would have been a state guest by now.

SHAKARA: Let them dare! Try me!

DUPE: Well, I'd be careful if I were you. The way you're going, the jail won't be far for too long.

SHAKARA: Try me? I'm ready!

DUPE: *(Bursting into laughter.)* Sha-ka-ra!

SHAKARA: *(Break-Dancing.)* Yeah, that's me. Dance-Hall Queen! *(DUPE changes the music and turns up the volume. The girls do an erotic dance movement.)*

DUPE: But that crook. What did he want?

SHAKARA: Ask me again. All he did was call out to Billy, his Alsatian dog. The dog simply stood in the centre of the crowd and started barking. Everyone fled. I scrambled to the gate, found myself alone. Without a car, I stood there numb and crippled as the party people flew across. Finally, as the DPO shut the door of the van behind me, he said to me "Goodnight, Miss. Be careful on your way. It's dark and dangerous." *(Pause.)* Fool! What's his business if I rise or fall?

DUPE: He's the DPO. Divisional Police Officer. The peoples' care-taker.

SHAKARA: He may be an undertaker for all I care. Let him go and crash. Took the milk-bottle right off...

DUPE: The babe's mouth, I know. Don't worry. Too bad. You missed.

SHAKARA: Always.

DUPE: There will always be another victim.

SHAKARA: When?

DUPE: Pray. Always...another victim.

SHAKARA: Who?

DUPE: Could be me. Could be you. Nobody is safe anymore.

SHAKARA: Woe betide my next...

DUPE: Mind you become your own victim.

SHAKARA: Then I'll have no regrets.

DUPE: Don't be so sure.

SHAKARA: I know myself.

DUPE: No. You don't! *(They are swinging, laughing, holding onto each other as in a tug-of-war.)*

SHAKARA: I promise. The next hawk will be shot; point-blank. No mercy! *(They laugh.)*

DUPE: *(Marching and singing.)* "We are soldiers..."

SHAKARA: *(Joining her.)* "We are soldiers. Fighting for our freedom. In the name of Jesus, we shall conquer!"

DUPE: *(Suddenly screams.)* The bloody mother!

SHAKARA: That woman is smart. Very smart.

DUPE: Too smart for her own good. Dangerously smart.

SHAKARA: The kind of woman we want nowadays. They're the best survivors.

DUPE: We want activists.

SHAKARA: Nonsense. Who feeds on activism? What for?

DUPE: Me. For me. We...women need to change this stinking world. We must.

SHAKARA: "Monkey dey work, baboon dey chop." No wonder your mother calls you "Acada."

DUPE: Yes, Acada-Bookworm. Anything wrong with that?

SHAKARA: Nothing. Except that academics have empty pockets. No. Leaking pockets, at best.

DUPE: So let them be. I prefer them to keep my sanity.

SHAKARA: Lunacy, you mean? People without money and too many books distress me.

DUPE: With that kind of disposition, you'll either end up in a hospital or in jail. Choose.

SHAKARA: Anyone will do. So long as I can get money. Money speaks.

DUPE: *(Laughing.)* A deadly language.

SHAKARA: Your mother knows. I love her guts.

DUPE: Happy to miss you. Good luck.

70

SHAKARA: *(Enchanted.)* You should have seen the way she cruised into our place with that Chief after you left.

DUPE: Crooks. All of them. What were they doing in your place anyway? Harassing that poor mother again?

SHAKARA: What do you expect? And do you blame them? *(Pause.)* Which of those men do you think your mom would end up with: The Chief or the DPO?

DUPE: How do I know? Ask her. I'm not her police, am I?

SHAKARA: Well, you should ask.

DUPE: For what?

SHAKARA: Look who's talking. Aren't you hungry for knowledge anymore?

DUPE: Not her. Not her type.

SHAKARA: It might help. I know she's well guarded. You should see her strides. *(Imitating.)* Oh, girl, that woman walks with such confidence!

DUPE: She thinks she's some goddess. Bitch-Goddess. Molesting everybody. Just because...my God! *(Sing-song.)* One of these days, she's gonna pay dearly! *(Pause.)* Why is she always molesting others?

SHAKARA: Who?

DUPE: Your mother, for example. What has she done to her? Sucker!

SHAKARA: We all suck. It's her own business.

DUPE: My mother's. I hate...

SHAKARA: What about her friend, the police officer?

DUPE: Uncle Shanka?

SHAKARA: Yes, that DPO. *(Thinking.)* Seems you hate the man too.

DUPE: Just one thing you got right.

SHAKARA: So why do you call him Uncle...?

DUPE: Forced. My mother insists that I call him that out of respect. She says that man knows everything about her life. I mean, *Everything!*

SHAKARA: *(Pensive.)* I see.

DUPE: What?

SHAKARA: Oh, nothing. Just don't know why they're so glued to each other, always.

DUPE: The man is our neighbor too.

SHAKARA: *(Alarmed.)* Is he?

DUPE: Yes. *(Silence.)* Does that bother you?

SHAKARA: Hnm...ye...not really...but...

DUPE: What?

SHAKARA: The nightclub...yes. You know that man is always around the nightclubs.

DUPE: Uncle Shanka? He's everywhere. Especially nowadays with his new promotion to the headquarters.

SHAKARA: As what?

DUPE: The new Director for Operation Sweep Clean. *(Again, they revert to play-acting.)*

SHAKARA: *(Loudly.)* Sweep the nation, under!

DUPE: Clean sweep, idiots!

SHAKARA: Dirt for the Po-lice!

DUPE: Death!

SHAKARA: For their partners!

DUPE: Operation Sweep!

SHAKARA: Sweep anyone who's scaring me away from my source of livelihood.

DUPE: Bless them. They're doing their job.

SHAKARA: Wrecking lives!

DUPE: Without them, with greedy mouths like you, the nation dies.

SHAKARA: In debt...

DUPE: *(Loudly.)* In dirt! What's the matter with you?

SHAKARA: *(Laughing.)* What's wrong with the world? Who cares?

DUPE: Some of us do...

72

SHAKARA: Perish!

DUPE: In the end, we all regret. All of us.

SHAKARA: After I get my share. That's all.

DUPE: Good luck! *(Play-acting ends. DUPE turns on her music. The girls sing and dance until DUPE suddenly stops and screams.)* I hate him! I hate them! But I'm trapped. You know that's why I started smoking and running to the clubs?

SHAKARA: You daredevil! I thought you enjoyed it.

DUPE: I try to...but, oh well. Forget it. Nothing matters anymore. I don't care if my Mom goes to hang herself if she can't stand me. It's my life, not hers.

SHAKARA: But why? You're so hard on your mother. Why?

DUPE: I don't have a mother. I wish...*(Sighing.)* Oh, Shak. If only...I knew...*(Silence. Suddenly she drops the question.)* How does it feel to grow up without a father?

SHAKARA: You know we're a family.

DUPE: Your father divorced your mother. *(Tearfully.)* But you know, I don't even know who my own father is.

SHAKARA: *(Cuddling her.)* Baby, I know what you mean. *(Silence.)*

DUPE: I keep imagining which of her business associates, so called, might be...you know. Any man could have been my father. I could walk past my own father and not even know it. Sad, isn't it?

SHAKARA: I understand. But your mother? She makes up for that.

DUPE: Selfish woman! So indulgent. *(Sobbing.)* Oh, Shak! You don't...can't understand. Nobody else does. It's just my problem and I've got to deal with it, somehow. *(Pensive.)* Sometimes, I've even wondered if it's that man...

SHAKARA: Who?

DUPE: Our neighbor.

SHAKARA: The Shanka-man, DPO? How come?

73

DUPE: Well, the way he stares? Burrowing so deep into my eyes...like...like...and you know? He'll do whatever I ask. Anything. Anytime Mom and I have an argument, she sends for him.

SHAKARA: And his wife and children?

DUPE: Somewhere, in some city. *(Sighing.)* Oh, Shak. At times, I think...I see myself in that man's eyes. Maybe that's why I seem to hate...him...*(Choking.)* At... at times, the way he treats me like his own? Just makes me long...*(Silence.)* Could that be my father?

SHAKARA: Ask your Mom? She knows.

DUPE: *(Sighs.)* Right. She alone can tell. *(Silence.)*

SHAKARA: Only mothers know who their baby's father is.

DUPE: *(Sobbing.)* That's why I keep running from nightclub to nightclub, just to kill the pain.

SHAKARA: Like me? Ha! *(She takes out two cigarettes and offers one to DUPE, whose awkward handling of it shows that she's still learning the art. DUPE pulls out her pillowcases, starts stuffing and dressing them like mannequins. SHAKARA assists her.)* Have you asked your mother?

DUPE: A million times! But the woman is so clever. Each time I ask, she changes the subject or tells me not to worry. Next, she goes and buys me some expensive presents to bribe me. Bribe! Bribery and corruption. That's all my mother knows. I bet she thinks she can bribe God too. Bribe her way right into heaven. Does she know that woman can't...live by bread alone?

SHAKARA: *(Giggling.)* And man can?

DUPE: Stop being frivolous! It's my own life I'm talking about, you know. Can't you see the boil...the sum total of my life?

SHAKARA: Every life, my dear! My sister calls it the 'cross.' Everyone carries one.

DUPE: Do I have to? Shak, mine's too heavy. I can't bear it anymore.

SHAKARA: *(Teasing.)* Then give it to me. Take mine.

DUPE: Won't you stop? Your laughter stabs...*(Voice cracking.)* Knife...in my heart...*(Suddenly.)* Shak, why are you like this?

SHAKARA: Like what?

DUPE: So...so free. Unserious? Friends should save. Not stab. It hurts. How can you be laughing when I confess my pain?

SHAKARA: It's my sin. I too have. My laughter is my confession. No. I confess in my laughter. To bear mine. Take it or leave it. *(Changing the subject.)* Ha! Ha! Ha! Fun time! Let's go to the Club.

DUPE: Why are you so vulgar? I'm dead serious.

SHAKARA: Then be dead! *(Chuckling.)* You're too serious about this God-forsaken life. That's what's the matter with you. Too serious. Your sin. Confess to Mother Shak.

DUPE: Giddy-goat-fool!

SHAKARA: *(Laughing.)* Then hers! *(She grabs the mannequin, swings it around and the stuffing comes apart.)* My God! She's done...undone! *(Frantically rocking DUPE, who's turned away.)* Dupe, she's come apart! Won't you help?

DUPE: *(Yelling.)* What?

SHAKARA: The mannequin!

DUPE: Your fault! Go figure it out and leave me alone. *(Hissing and cursing under her breath, SHAKARA bends down to pick up the pieces. But she's nauseated and running between the toilet and the parlor to pick up scattered pieces of the mannequin on the floor. DUPE, too, is disgusted. She wanders off to a corner of the room and explodes.)* Where do I go? Who is my father? Where is he? What am I going to do? I have nobody. I'm alone. I'm lost. *(Singing the blues.)*

SHAKARA: *(Crosses over to lean on and rub DUPE's back.)* I've got it all together now. Don't be so sad. Can't you see you're not alone anymore? We're in this together.

DUPE: Are we?

SHAKARA: Hold me. *(DUPE obeys.)* I'm ready. Tomorrow, it will shine. Better tomorrow. That's what my mother says.

DUPE: You believe her?

SHAKARA: Sometimes.

DUPE: I do, always.

SHAKARA: Then let's go.

DUPE: Take. Fly freedom-child! All I want now is my Prince. *(Loud laughter.)*

SHAKARA: A prince, trapped in another woman's body. Ha! *(DUPE dials the phone and invites PRINCE to come with her to the nightclub. She drops the phone with a long sigh.)*

DUPE: The dog...

SHAKARA: Coming?

DUPE: Not there.

SHAKARA: So where...?

DUPE: Who knows where the so-called loved ones are when you need them most? *(Sighs again.)* It's time. Let's go. *(Suddenly, the door cracks open. They hide under the sofa. Frightened and peeping through the window.)* Alawo, is that you?

THE GUARD/ALAWO: Beeni, Sissy Dupe. Na Oga...

DUPE: *(Alarmed.)* Which Oga?

THE GUARD/ALAWO: Your man, de Oga.

DUPE: Oh, you mean Prince?

THE GUARD/ALAWO: Beeni, Sissy. *(Still panting, SHAKARA re-emerges from her hideout, no longer afraid.)*

DUPE: *(Opening the front door.)* My darling! *(She kisses her PRINCE, then turns to THE GUARD/ALAWO.)* Here, Alawo. Take this money and stay on guard. Just in case...

THE GUARD/ALAWO: Mommy?

DUPE: Yes. Stay awake. Let me know. You know that woman.

THE GUARD/ALAWO: Sissy, God go bless you!

DUPE: Amen. *(Exit GUARD, DUPE shuts the door and she kisses PRINCE again.)* Oh, God! Drunk as a fish again? *(PRINCE is giggling and staggering.)* Here, greet my friend Shakara.

PRINCE: *(Staggering.)* So this is it...*(Hiccups.)* Shak...Sha-ka-ra...? *(Offering a bottle.)* Hey, what can I do you for, my lady Shark? You're lonely, I can see...

SHAKARA: You can?

PRINCE: Sure. Don't worry. I'll hook you up with...

SHAKARA: *(Excitedly.)* Somebody? With money? Where's he?

PRINCE: Easy girl. Trust me. *(PRINCE is about to light a cigarette, but DUPE stops him.)*

DUPE: Mommy!

PRINCE: The virgin?

DUPE: Yes, virginia! *(They laugh. PRINCE ignores her warning and starts puffing away at his cigarette.)*

PRINCE: Easy girl. That will be arranged.

SHAKARA: Oh, Dupe! Who is it?

PRINCE: Somebody. A friend.

DUPE: I told you.

PRINCE: *(Nudging SHAKARA. Belching.)* You know...the DPO?

DUPE: *(Hissing.)* Dat nozy man. *Busy-body die for gutter!*

SHAKARA: *(Excitedly.)* Yes! Hook me...hook me up!

PRINCE: With him? Soon. You'll see. His son, my bosom friend...*(Belching.)* Abroad. Soon come...

DUPE: I like him, not his father though.

PRINCE: That dog! Always sniffing into everybody's business. One of these days, he's gonna get trapped.

DUPE: By whom?

PRINCE: *(Chuckling.)* You, of course! *(Pause.)* Don't worry. Could be you. Could be me. Her. Anybody. God works in mysterious ways. That DPO thinks he's a smart guy, but he's really dumb. His son is in business with...some big time 419 criminal and he doesn't even know it.

DUPE: Tell me, who's he?

PRINCE: Never mind. They're people you know too well.

DUPE: Don't tell me it's the Chief Chairman and...

PRINCE: Your Mom, of course!

DUPE: Ah, I should have known! *(Sighs.)*

SHAKARA: When is he coming back?

PRINCE: Soon.

SHAKARA: I can't wait.

DUPE: *(Opening a bottle of alcohol.)* Let's celebrate!

PRINCE: *(Drinking heavily.)* Yeah, to youth and life! Away with parents!

DUPE: Away with authorities!

SHAKARA: We've been waiting too long. Let's go!

PRINCE: *(Still drinking, tipsy.)* Silly goose! Freedom-child! Let's celebrate! *(Loud music as they dance some provocative dance-steps. Still visibly drunk as they sing and dance, PRINCE holds on tightly to DUPE and yells.)* Girl, I want you!

DUPE: Oh no! Not now! *(Briefly hums.)* "No-No-No baby not now." A Gentleman must learn to wait.

PRINCE: Gentleman in waiting? Ha!

DUPE: Got it!

PRINCE: It's almost time for the show. You need a ride?

DUPE: No, thanks. Got it all under control.

SHAKARA: So?

DUPE: "No cause for control. Everything is under alarm!" *(They laugh.)*

PRINCE: *(Staggering to the door.)* Got ya! *(A group hug. The girls escort him out. Blackout. Followed with a slow spotlight on DUPE and SHAKARA waiting anxiously as DUPE searches for something,)*

SHAKARA: Dupe, let's go. I'm scared!

DUPE: *(Still searching.)* Again?

SHAKARA: Your Moth...Let's get out of here before she comes.

DUPE: We still have time. I'm in charge here. I can't go 'til I find the keys.

SHAKARA: *(Alarmed.)* My God. Her car keys?

DUPE: Of course! Baby, stay cool. What do bitches do except bark and yell? *(Barking.)* Don't worry. We're cruising there in a big way.

SHAKARA: *(Warming up.)* True?

DUPE: Trust me. God, show me the key! *(Searches.)* Hey key, where are you? You better show up before this woman comes.

SHAKARA: *(They pull out all the drawers.)* Oh, key. Come now-Come-now. Please come now-now. *(Together, they continue searching until DUPE stumbles on the bunch of keys.)*

DUPE: Eureka! I found it!

SHAKARA: *(Chanting.)* "Tonite is the night!"

DUPE: Gondola, here we come! Come! Meet Freedom-Child! Are you ready? We gonna make it tonite!

SHAKARA: Yes, but...*(SHAKARA stands stuttering and staring at her feet.)* My... shoes. *(DUPE stops, surveys SHAKARA from head to toe. Laughs.)*

DUPE: Girl, that wig? You look like a mop!

SHAKARA: You think it's funny to be with...out...?

DUPE: *(Offering her a pair of shoes.)* Okay. Stop whining. Try these.

SHAKARA: *(Tries, gives up.)* They don't fit.

DUPE: *(Chuckling as she offers her a red pair of shoes.)* Here. I'm sure you'd love...

SHAKARA: *(Apprehensive.)* Yours?

DUPE: Hers.

SHAKARA: *(Alarmed.)* Your mother's shoes?

DUPE: *(Laughing.)* Wear them. *Paw-fect* fit.

SHAKARA: *(Taking up the shoes.)* My friend, you want to kill me?

DUPE: *(Laughing.)* Trust me. Girl, you got your dreams right in your hands. Count yourself as chosen, lucky one. You asked for it. And you got it! *(In utter disbelief, SHAKARA stares at her feet, her hands and the shoes.)*

SHAKARA: *(Trembling.)* But...you're...sure this...this won't land me in trouble?

DUPE: *(Playfully.)* So you are scared too? But you've lived all your life courting trouble?

SHAKARA: Risk. It's risky...

DUPE: *(Giggling.)* Your middle name! Not so? Ha! *(With trembling hands, SHAKARA steps into the shoes.)*

SHAKARA: *(Resolved.)* Oh well, whatever. *(Chanting.)* Let it-let it be-let it be! Life is...

DUPE: Risky!

SHAKARA: The roads are...

DUPE: *(Exhilarated.)* Risqué!

SHAKARA: We live by faith. That's what Mama said. *(Resolved, SHAKARA puts on the shoes, struts around as she admires herself in front of the standing mirror.)*

DUPE: *(Chuckling.)* You daredevil! See now? They match.

SHAKARA: The shoes?

DUPE: *(Teasing.)* Your feet, (h)idiot!

SHAKARA: *(Sighing.)* But...your mother!

DUPE: *(Giddy.)* Won't be missed. Time up!

SHAKARA: Sure?

DUPE: Positive. Time. Life is short.

SHAKARA: *(Laughing.)* "So eat dessert first!" That's what I learnt in that Catholic boarding school.

DUPE: Where you got messed up?

SHAKARA: I went to school.

DUPE: But did school go through you? Ha!

SHAKARA: My God, the shoe...!

DUPE: What has God got to do with it? Come girl. Wear the shoes and leave the poor old God alone. You people trouble that God too much. *(Bending over.)* That woman will soon earn her reward.

SHAKARA: Not while I'm here. Let's go.

DUPE: You ready for battle?

SHAKARA: Yeeess!

DUPE: No, you're not!

SHAKARA: I am.

DUPE: You got your rain-coat?

SHAKARA: What for? It's not raining yet.

DUPE: Oh yes, it is! Inside. Raining all the time. Every sensible woman knows. But not you, Shak. Until you get some sense knocked into you, maybe.

SHAKARA: You've lost me completely.

DUPE: We'll find out. *(Pause.)* I'm getting you a Life-Jacket to protect you from those live bullets.

SHAKARA: What the hell are you talking about?

DUPE: Life! Better be armed. Then you won't drown. Indeed, that's how to swim, afloat. *(DUPE takes out a small plastic case from her mother's drawer, gives SHAKARA a rubber pouch.)*

SHAKARA: Are you drunk or what?

DUPE: Well, try it. Afterwards, tell me if I'm drunk.

SHAKARA: *(Curiously.)* What the hell is this?

DUPE: *(Laughing.)* (H)idiot! You want to run. But you have no feet? Ha! Tell me how you're now going to cry without eyes?

SHAKARA: DD, stop speaking in tongues like my damned saintly sister and tell me what I need to know. *(Staring at the object.)* What is this thing?

81

DUPE: You'll soon find out. Just take it to the bathroom.

SHAKARA: What for?

DUPE: *(Teasing, laughing.)* Ajèè kpako!

SHAKARA: Ajèè butter!

DUPE: I've told you. It's dangerous to be out there with those frogs without your raincoat. You don't want any excess baggage now. Do you?

SHAKARA: Me? Never! Free as a bird. That's what I want.

DUPE: Then get ready to fly. That thing, too, is hers.

SHAKARA: *(Alarmed.)* What?

DUPE: My mother's.

SHAKARA: God! Kill me quick!

DUPE: Hurry up now and put it on. I made sure I gave you one that's second new.

SHAKARA: *(Turning it over.)* But how does it fit?

DUPE: I know. My mother, extra large...*(Looks at the clock.)* Time to go. Hurry up!

SHAKARA: God save me! Show me...

DUPE: Ajèè kpako! I'll come with you. *(They disappear into the bathroom and re-appear shortly.)*

SHAKARA: *(Excitedly.)* Now I'm ready! I just can't wait.

DUPE: *(Pulling her chin.)* Patience!

SHAKARA: Too costly. Can't afford it now.

DUPE: What do they say? Ehm..."a patient dog eats the fattest bones."

SHAKARA: *(Giggling.)* No bones for me, now. Enough! *(Emphatically.)* All I ever want is my fair share; juicy, succulent flesh.

DUPE: *(Teasing.)* Shak, the terrific dog!

SHAKARA: No apologies. We gotta move on.

DUPE: Mind you break your jaw.

SHAKARA: Too bad. All I want is my share. Exchange is no robbery. Remember?

DUPE: I guess.

SHAKARA: I'm hungry.

DUPE: Hungry dog.

SHAKARA: Yeah. Angry dog.

DUPE: 'Shameless,' your middle name?

SHAKARA: No regrets!

DUPE: More shame!

SHAKARA: Woe betide any man that comes my way!

DUPE: *(Break-dancing.)* Kill them quick-quick! *(Play-acting mixed with erotic dance.)*

SHAKARA: Roll dem for ground.

DUPE: Quick!

SHAKARA: *(Aiming below.)* One-eyed-bullet!

DUPE: Shoot!

SHAKARA: Another robber has just fallen.

DUPE: *O'masheee-o*! A fallen hero! *(The phone rings. DUPE grabs it. SHAKARA is quite apprehensive.)*

SHAKARA: Who?

DUPE: My mother. Who else?

SHAKARA: She's on her way?

DUPE: No. Not now. She says she won't be back tonight. Something else came up.

SHAKARA: Hooray! Away with mothers! *(They drink and break into song as they march.)*

DUPE: *(Putting on her hot-pants.)* Armed to the teeth!

SHAKARA: Yeah, the only way. Make way, everybody! The bulldozers are here!

DUPE: Armed to the teeth. Watch out, man! Watch out for your pocket!

SHAKARA: Live bullets! Shoot! Shoot down the pocket. Obstructions out! Anything...

DUPE: Slowing down progress. *(Giggling like school girls playing and reciting, they speed up action in a call-re-*

sponse change. SHAKARA chases DUPE around to get back at her as they both retouch their make-up. But DUPE is swift and ducks her while they exchange throwing cosmetic items at each other.)

SHAKARA: You devil! Wait!

DUPE: Catch me if you can!

SHAKARA: Turn foxes at night. Watch out. Nocturnal animals grazing.

DUPE: Preying.

SHAKARA: Hunting.

DUPE: Lioness in search of food.

SHAKARA: *(Declamatory.)* Eat or be eaten! You Reverend Saints!

DUPE: I hate Saints!

SHAKARA: Why?

DUPE: Saints bore me.

SHAKARA: *(Laughing.)* Ugh-ugh...Saints and reverends. Beware, the wolves are here!

DUPE: They're coming...coming too! Ugh-Ugh-Ugh! Beware! Saints and Reverends! *(The girls parody the Nuns. They start play-acting, DUPE as the nun.)* 'Girls, time to lock up! Every student must be in bed once the lights go out! Time out!'

SHAKARA: *(Closing the door and reopening it once "Sister" leaves.)* Indeed! Time out, Sister Margaret!

DUPE: *(Chuckling.)* I hear you. *(Light dims. "Sister" returns to the convent. SHAKARA hurriedly takes off her school uniform and changes into a short, seductive, glittering nightclub dress. KECHI or PRINCE can play the role of the NIGHT-CALLER. Hushed male voice calling to get in: "Sue open. Open Sue. Wake up, sweet Suzie! Wake up!" Sweet Suzie song in the background. SHAKARA opens the door. NIGHT-CALLER sneaks into the dormitory. Boy and girl dance and swing bosom to bosom. Boy kisses and disappears under the bed-sheet. Mixed music and snoring in the background followed by funny rocking sounds. They rise. Boy leaves. Next, girl dresses up the pillow in her school uniform. The pillow now looks like a mannequin. Hugging the mannequin, she whispers, "Sleep baby. I'll be back." She covers up the 'pillow-girl/ mannequin' with her bed-sheet. Kisses the 'pillow-girl' goodbye as they leave for the nightclub, shutting the door behind them. Long after midnight, lover girl returns tired and yawning. She pulls off her party dress, gives the dummy 'pillow-girl' a congratulatory pat on the back and pulls off the bed-covers with a smile and a victory sign to her lover, who salutes: "Now Sister Margaret. Goodnight, and see you tomorrow!" Play-acting over, the girls explode into laughter.)* Girl, that's how to survive in today's world where the enemy is at large. And you got no power.

DUPE: Nor cover.

SHAKARA: Wear ten faces.

DUPE: You dance the "fox-trot" as I do here to survive my mother's tyranny.

SHAKARA: Girl, you think you're alone. I'm with you to the end!

DUPE: The tyranny of parents?

SHAKARA: They think they're clever.

DUPE: We'll teach them!

SHAKARA: Show them!

SHAKARA & DUPE: *(Together.)* Show them! Show them! These busy-body mothers and fathers! Show them-show-them these busy-body parents!

DUPE: *(Alone, to the audience.)* Yes, countrymen and women. My mother thinks she knows everything. What should I do with her? *(Awaiting response.)* Does she know how often my Prince sneaks in here to sleep with me? HA!

SHAKARA: Ooh-la-lah! How can?

DUPE: *(Seductively.)* Yes, my Prince. He comes, I feel him coming.

SHAKARA: *(Teasing, laughing.)* Like twice a month?

85

DUPE: You crazy? Like every hour!

SHAKARA: *(Amuzed, she throws herself on the floor.)* Girl, you're blessed with a coming-machine? So help me, God. *(SHAKARA kneels at DUPE's feet. Acting the priestess with a bottle of alcohol in hand. DUPE 'baptizes' the supplicant as she chants: "Dominus Vomitus?" The baptized answers "Amen!"*

DUPE: Rise daughter. Your faith has saved you. You survived the downpour.

SHAKARA: "Reign of Terror!"

DUPE: No. The "Rain" of terror. That's what they mean.

SHAKARA: Yes, baptized by fire!

DUPE: Ha! When I turn up the music and my mother thinks it's the late-night slow-jam? *(Demonstrating.)* And so we dig it-dig-dig-it and dig it...

SHAKARA: And smoke. *(Suddenly, SHAKARA raises a mock alarm, imitating MADAM KOFO's voice." Who's there? Dupe! Dupe, my baby! Where are you baby?" DUPE jumps to light up the incense and to stuff several peppermints sweets into her mouth. Silence, except for the sounds of snoring. Satisfied, the imaginary 'Madam Kofo' returns to her bed, sighing, "Poor child. She's fast asleep!" End of role-playing.)*

SHAKARA: Waooooooooo! Girl, you'll out-play the devil in her own game. I troway salute. *(They exchange a clapping salute.)*

DUPE: Practice makes...

SHAKARA: *Paw-feet!*

DUPE: Let's make it. *(DUPE checks around to see if everything is in place.)*

SHAKARA: But what if your mother...

DUPE: Comes? I know she will. But I'm always so much ahead of her. The guard, Alawo, is brother man.

SHAKARA: The grand 'cover-up.'

DUPE: Damn it! Must we say it all?

SHAKARA: *(Laughing.)* Oh no-oh yes! We accept...your 'confidant!'

DUPE: Good. Let's go. *(They move to the doorway.)*

SHAKARA: You owe your life to that guard.

DUPE: Don't I know it? And that's why I always like to treat him right. Give him a lot of presents.

SHAKARA: Hail, Holy-Theif! By stealing your mother's rice to give him and cook?

DUPE: Yes. She'd never know. She has so much she won't know the difference.

SHAKARA: So you think, Miss Santa Claus. Let her catch you giving away her property. You think everyday is Christmas? Everyday is for the thief. One day is for the owner.

DUPE: But see? I'm armed. Let her try. *(Flexing her muscles and humming a tune. "It's time-time-time...Catch me if you can!" SHAKARA stands in front of the mirror to admire herself as she struts.)*

SHAKARA: A new me? Great! *(Shouting.)* Are you ready! Armed. Got my boots!

DUPE: Got life-proof-jacket! Shoot!

SHAKARA: *(Shoots at the imaginary target.)* Tooooooooooooom! *(DUPE now holding two inflated balloons, gives one to SHAKARA.)*

DUPE: *(Chanting.)* Blow-Blow girl! Blow! Now! *(Together, they blow. The balloons either burst or get deflated as they blow.*

SHAKARA & DUPE: *(Together.)* Bravo! At last! Night is calling. Gondola, here we come! *(They exit hand-in-hand, swinging and singing, "We gonna dance! We gonna jive! We gonna party tonite!" Blackout.)*

THE SEVENTH STAGE

The Streets Have Claws

(Dawn is approaching. SHAKARA and DUPE stagger into MADAM KOFO's bed room. They are drunk, disheveled, with PRINCE staggering behind them. They trip and fall.)

DUPE: *(Clinging to PRINCE.)* Over.

PRINCE: *(Hiccups.)* Over. It's over.

SHAKARA: *(Nudging him.)* Come. Let's do it before *Lady High-Heel...* (Singing).

PRINCE: *(Croaking a song behind her.)* Comes. She's coming. Coming to-mor-row!

SHAKARA: *(Trembling, falling.)* Is she? But you said...she's lost.

DUPE: *(Kicking her.)* Gone, dummy! The devil gonna get ya!

SHAKARA: Ready. Take me! I wanna be...with my God...go back...

DUPE: *(Sing-song.)* Tooo-mor-row!

PRINCE: *(Laughing, stripping the 'mannequin.')* See! She's naked.

SHAKARA: Who is? *(Taking the mannequin from the giggling PRINCE.)*

DUPE: She, zombie!

SHAKARA: Your mother! Undone? Ha! Ha! Ha! She's coming...

DUPE: Damn it! She's gone...(She snatches it from her.)

PRINCE: Naked.

DUPE: Aren't we all?

SHAKARA: Your mouth will soon kill you.

DUPE: One way or the other. Something kills...

SHAKARA: I understand.

DUPE: What do you understand? Ehn?

SHAKARA: My dream. One thing I'm sure of.

DUPE: *(Laughing.)* Another life. Never to come back.

PRINCE: Gone?

DUPE: Forever.

PRINCE: Sleep. It's time.

DUPE: Short. Life is short.

SHAKARA: So eat dessert first! *(They laugh. DUPE gives SHAKARA a nightgown, a cap and other sleeping items as PRINCE produces a bottle of alcohol which he serves everyone.)*

PRINCE: *(Toasting.)* To us who can...

SHAKARA: Drink!

DUPE: To the dying...

PRINCE: To us!

SHAKARA: The Living!

DUPE: Dead! *(Clinking glasses.)*

PRINCE: *(Offering his to the 'mannequin.')* Drink to her! *(They drink. The girls are increasingly tipsy and fall on each other. PRINCE falls between them, pumping and squeezing whatever he's able to hold onto. SHAKARA moans.)*

SHAKARA: Love it - Love it! Life is good.

DUPE: Hurts! It hurts! Stop it, you! *(Spanks PRINCE.)*

PRINCE: *(Humming.)* "No woman, no cry. No woman, no cry..." *(DUPE turns her back and feigns snoring. He turns to SHAKARA who is enjoying the game. But DUPE intercepts his hands or legs each time they move in SHA-KARA's direction. Giving up, PRINCE falls asleep and starts snoring. Suddenly, a car pulls up at the gate.)*

SHAKARA: *(Springing up.)* She's here! I'm dead!

DUPE: *(Alarmed.)* Who?

SHAKARA: *(Terrified.)* Your Mother!

DUPE: The devil! Run! Disappear! *(With lightening speed, SHAKARA flings the cover, grabs her shoes, and holds them to her bosom as she flees into the next room. Every other thing has been abandoned on top of the dresser with the standing mirror. Meanwhile, DUPE is busy trying to get PRINCE to wake up and escape. But PRINCE is already far gone. The alcohol with cigarette smoke boasts their presence all around. DUPE is increasingly desperate as she shakes him.)* Come on! Wake up! She's here!

PRINCE: *(Snorting.)* Who...the devil? What? I hear the devil. *(Drunkenly.)* Out! You devil you! Out of the way! *(Car engine is running. Sounds of honking at the gate. Voices outside. Frantic, DUPE slaps his backside, but he simply turns and falls back into loud snoring. More agitated now, DUPE tries to lift him up and force his eyes open.)*

DUPE: Oh, God! You're the biggest devil, shut your foul mouth. Rise! Come with me. Now! *(She yanks his limbs a few more times.)*

PRINCE: *(Staggering, stammering.)* What? Want me...to come...now? *(Loud belching.)* Can't...come. Not now. *(Belching again.)*

DUPE: *(Pulling him.)* Come, Prince. My Mother!

PRINCE: *(Groggily.)* Your Mama coming? Great! Then let her come and leave me alone. *(He falls back on the floor and starts snoring again. More desperate, DUPE yanks his foot forward. He resists, kicks her back. She tries again and fails as he protests and yells.)* What? What do you want?

DUPE: Come with me now.

PRINCE: *(Drunkenly.)* But I'm not...ready now. Need a...Viagra boost! Yeah! *(Belches.)*

DUPE: *(Rolling him over.)* Oh, come now! You son of a b...!

PRINCE: Yeah! I was born by a b...*(Hiccups.)* Now, what do you want?

DUPE: *(Threatening.)* I'm going to pour ice-water on you! Just wait.

PRINCE: *(Rising, staggering.)* I need it-I need it. Girl, baptize me...your love... *(PRINCE starts humming an old popular tune: "What do you want from me? Putting me in misery. Oh baby that's not Love. Will you please set me free!" As DUPE runs to fetch the ice-water, the screen shows flashes of the scene outside.)*

MADAM KOFO: *(Outside.)* Okay, darling! Tomorrow then. *(Seductively.)* Dream of me. Sweet dreams!

CHIEF CHAIRMAN: See you tomorrow. Goodnight!

MADAM KOFO: *(Approaching the front door.)* Goodnight, my love. *(Brief silence.)* Alawo! Where are you? *(The GUARD/ALAWO is still confused.)*

THE GUARD/ALAWO: Here Mo!

MADAM KOFO: What the hell are you waiting for? Why's the gate not open?

THE GUARD/ALAWO: *(Nervously.)* Ah, k'osi ma. Notin. Notin, Mo...

MADAM KOFO: Then why do you keep standing there like 'Soldier Idumota?' Be quick and open the damned thing!

THE GUARD/ALAWO: *(Nervously.)* Be'eni ma. Yes, Mo...I go *(h)*open...*(He is fidgeting and pretending that he has misplaced the key.)* E no dey gree *(h)*open, Ma.

MADAM KOFO: What?

THE GUARD/ALAWO: *(Kicking at the gate.)* Na wetin dey do dis door now? Not today man pickin begin *(h)*open sometin? Ehn? I beg, *(h)*open, joooo! Wetin?

MADAM KOFO: *(Threatening.)* You, me-guard! Get ready for your obituary!

THE GUARD/ALAWO: *(Alarmed.)* Me die? God no go agree. No vex, Mo. *(Pause. Starts running towards the house.)* Na Sissy. Yes! I dey go call Sissy Dupe to *(h)*open am with him own key. My own no dey work well. E dey bend, small-small. Sometime self, E day jam for *(h)*inside. Wait Mo. I dey come now-now! *(He runs towards the front door, whispers.)* Sissy! Sissy Dupe! E don happen-

91

o! Come! Quick-Quick! *(No answer. He kicks at the door as a way of signaling to DUPE and her friends. Spotlights reveal the scene inside. Meanwhile, inside, DUPE desperately yanks PRINCE's foot forward, but only the shoe string yields to her. For a moment, she stands staring at the shoe string. Hisses, throws it down, and pulls at the other foot. PRINCE is kicking at her as she pulls. After so many trials, DUPE finally pulls him into the closet and locks him up. Outside, the GUARD/ALAWO continues his own struggles.)*

MADAM KOFO: *(Flashes the light outside.)* What should one do with so many idiots around? Common door, you can't even open? Imagine if a robber came here and I had to escape. Ehn? Out! Out of my way! What do we have here? A mouse or a man? *(Silence as THE GUARD/ ALAWO struggles with the key.)* Alawo, are you a man at all?

THE GUARD/ALAWO: *(Fondling another door to get DUPE's attention.)* No! Oh, yes...yes ma! I be man. Proper-proper. True, my wife go swear for me! Allah! *(Kicking at the door.)* Just sake of dis gate dey pepper me. My own key don bend. You know say eferytin don dark well-well for (h)inside.

MADAM KOFO: Idiot! Then turn on the lights!

THE GUARD/ALAWO: Yes Mo. I forget. Na Sissy Dupe own I take (h)open am before-before. *(Calling.)* Sissy Dupe! Sissy! De key. (H)open! Quick-Quick! *(Silence.)*

MADAM KOFO: *(Impatiently.)* Why are you waking her up? Leave my innocent child alone. She's sleeping. Not responsible for your carelessness. Is she?

THE GUARD/ALAWO: *(Stuttering.)* Yes Mo...Ah, no Mo!

MADAM KOFO: I just can't believe this. Alawo, are you planning to rob me?

THE GUARD/ALAWO: Otioooo! Never!

MADAM KOFO: That's what you all say. If the key was bad, why didn't you tell me?

THE GUARD/ALAWO: I swear Mo. Na (h)only dis night. Just

dis night de tin kpafuka.

MADAM KOFO: Idiot! You think you can fool me?

THE GUARD/ALAWO: Ah, no. God forbid bad tin-o!

MADAM KOFO: Or you think I'll be gone forever?

THE GUARD/ALAWO: *(Muttering and fiddling.)* Yes...No...yes Mo...

MADAM KOFO: *(Stunned.)* What? What did you say? Say that again and you're fired!

THE GUARD/ALAWO: *(Frantic, he starts to unlock the gate.)* Fire? No! Wetin? I no talk anytin ma. Notin. Notin at all-at all. Na *(h)*only say my own key come jam for today and na Sissy Dupe *(h)*own I come use to *(h)*open am. *(Louder.)* Make you no vex, Mo! Goodnight ma! *(No response, only the sound of MADAM KOFO's high-heeled shoes approaching the door. The doorknob turns, and MADAM KOFO pushes the door open. DUPE has finally succeeded in pulling PRINCE out of the way and hidden the mess littered on the floor. As soon as her mother enters, DUPE jumps to stand on top of PRINCE's shoes as she greets her mother quite warmly to mask her nervousness.)*

DUPE: Mommsie, you're back!

MADAM KOFO: *(Startled.)* So you're still awake?

DUPE: Yes, Mommy. I was watching a late night movie.

MADAM KOFO: I see. *(Pause.)* And missing Mommy?

DUPE: Sure, Mommsie.

MADAM KOFO: *(Fondling DUPE's hair.)* My sweet baby. It's so nice to hear that fond name again. *(Repeating.)* 'Mommsie.' Great! It's been such a long time since you addressed me so affectionately. Is everything okay?

DUPE: Sure! Sure Mom. You know things are never the same when you're not here.

MADAM KOFO: *(Relaxing, taking off her shoes.)* I know dear. Come, baby. Sit here on Mommy's lap. *(At first, DUPE hesitates.)*

DUPE: But Mommy, I'm not a child anymore. Don't you fear

I'll break your foot or spine?

MADAM KOFO: *(Yawning.)* A child is never too big for her parent. Okra never grows bigger than its planter. Come. You know this is the best moment we're having in a very long time?

DUPE: Oh, you parents and your trappings! *(Cautiously, she sits on her mother's lap as MADAM KOFO turns on a "slow-night jam." Running footsteps are heard as SHA-KARA now tries to escape through the backdoor. But it's locked and she throws herself behind the TV set. Her limbs are sticking out, but only DUPE can see.)*

MADAM KOFO: *(Suddenly apprehensive.)* What was that?

DUPE: *(Nervous.)* Nothing.

MADAM KOFO: It's footsteps. I heard footsteps.

DUPE: Oh, Mommsie. Must be the dogs playing.

MADAM KOFO: Hnm...Maybe.

DUPE: *(Cajoling her.)* Mommy, you look tired. Time to sleep.

MADAM KOFO: *(Yawning.)* Oh, no dear. There's still time. I'm okay. *(She sneezes, rises to get some tissue paper from the bathroom opposite, but DUPE already double-crosses her.)*

DUPE: *(Running to fetch it.)* Relax Mommy. I'll get it...anything you ask now. Rest!

MADAM KOFO: *(Loudly.)* My Angel! Please boil some water in the kettle. I'm so stressed out and fatigued. I need some hot tea to soothe my aching nerves.

DUPE: *(Chuckling.)* That you need, Mommy!

MADAM KOFO: Thank you, dear. I'm so proud of you. And I'm so glad I raised you to be this way. *(DUPE gives her the tissue. She blows her nose.)* The flu? Maybe.

DUPE: Drink some brandy?

MADAM KOFO: Oh no, darling. That will weaken me further.

DUPE: But that's what you normally drink when...

MADAM KOFO: Yes, dear. But not for this kind of...*(Pause.)* I think it's my allergy. I'll be okay soon. *(Stretching.)* Oh, dear. I've been gone for so long, I've lost track...*(Pause.)* Who knows what's going on in this crazy land? Let's hear the news. *(Goes to turn on the TV set. SHAKARA's limbs are still sticking out from under the huge TV set. DUPE quickly blocks her way and tries to distract her mother.)*

DUPE: Mommy, you shouldn't bother about what's going on.

MADAM KOFO: No, dear. I should. It's very important for me to know. Otherwise the whole world could be falling apart and I won't even have a clue.

DUPE: Such things don't matter now. Mom, go to bed. Don't tire yourself out anymore. *(MADAM KOFO insists on hearing the news. DUPE quickly goes over again, sits on SHAKARA's limbs to cover them up.)*

MADAM KOFO: I know, Angel. *(Yawns.)* The water is boiling. Go fetch the teapot.

DUPE: *(Very uneasy.)* Ehmmm...Mom...No. Not yet.

MADAM KOFO: But dear, the water is already boiling over. I can hear it. I need the tea...

DUPE: *(Rubbing her back.)* Mommsie, you know the thing with that electric kettle, anyway. Boils just too fast and too loud. It will shut itself off when it's yelled enough.

MADAM KOFO: *(Relishing the massage.)* Hnm. That feels so good! Yes, I hear you.

DUPE: When I know it's cooled enough, I'll serve the tea. I don't want you to get burnt.

MADAM KOFO: Neither do I, my Angel! Get my baby burnt? No, dear! I can wait...*(Pause. She hears SHAKARA groaning underneath.)* Dear, you seem to be uncomfortable. Are you alright?

DUPE: *(Exaggerated groans.)* Cramps, Mom. Just these nagging cramps.

MADAM KOFO: *(Concerned, bending over.)* Oh, dear! You

need some pain pill?

DUPE: *(Groaning, bending over.)* No, Mommy. But for such stubborn aches. Nothing helps, I'm afraid.

MADAM KOFO: *(Standing.)* I'll fetch you some. *(MADAM KOFO goes to get her handbag. Relieved, DUPE pushes SHAKARA's legs in and runs after her mother immediately. She gives DUPE the medication with a glass of water. DUPE pretends to be drinking, but throws the tablets over her head. Silence.)* You think you'll be okay? Otherwise, you'll have to see the doctor.

DUPE: *(Still pretending.)* No Mommy. I need no doctor now. *(Pause.)* I'm worried...just worried about you. If only you'd go to bed. I'll be okay.

MADAM KOFO: *(Affectionately.)* My dear, how sweet! So understanding! Soon, I'll go...sleep. But first, let me take my tea. *(She rises to fetch the hot kettle. PRINCE is snoring heavily now. MADAM KOFO hears the noise, listens.)* Strange!

DUPE: *(Nervously.)* What, Mommy?

MADAM KOFO: *(Sniffing the air.)* Hnm...A sound...a smell...?

DUPE: *(Distracting her.)* Oh, Mommy. It's all in your head. You're just tired. That's all. Go to bed.

MADAM KOFO: But the tea. Get me a cup and...

DUPE: *(Massaging her mother's shoulders.)* Soon, Mommy. Soon. *(Pause.)* You know, Mommy. It's been such a long time since we shared anything together. Now tell me about your trip.

MADAM KOFO: *(Turning down the TV.)* Oh, that? Beautiful. Excellent opportunity. It was great except for those wretched poor who try to ruin your day. *(Again she yawns, listens and sniffs the air.)* Hnm...something...I smell something...

DUPE: *(Quickly.)* It's nothing. Just the dog, fouling the air.

MADAM KOFO: My puppies? Are they okay?

DUPE: Everything is okay, Mom.

MADAM KOFO: As I was saying, dear, those lazy wretched poor are so sneaky and stubborn. I have no patience with them. Littering the entire place. *(Spits.)* Even in churches nowadays. They are there. Everywhere. Braying and calling on God. To do what? Save them. Bless them. Wipe out their poverty as if God is Director of the World Bank. And the IMF runs on charity. My dear, if you go to that border? Ah! The poor trading on miracles! I just don't know what this country is turning to. And the foolish government is not even doing anything about it.

DUPE: What do you want them to do?

MADAM KOFO: Ban them! Sweep them out! All of them!

DUPE: From where? To where?

MADAM KOFO: From everywhere; the churches, at least. And from certain respected areas where decent people live. I mean, it's an eyesore to come into the church nowadays and you can't find any room in the front seat. I tell you, it's becoming so annoying that our Merchants' Club is now raising some good money to put down for all the front seats in the church.

DUPE: Exclusively for your members?

MADAM KOFO: Yes, my dear. About time!

DUPE: I see. *(Silence.)*

MADAM KOFO: Just imagine. Before I left, I stopped by that wretch, Omesiete.

DUPE: Hnm. What has the poor woman done again? Aren't you tired?

MADAM KOFO: Of course I am. Tired! Tired of her nonsense. That's why she must pack out...*(Sniffing more.)* Something's smelling.

DUPE: *(Distracting her.)* Poor woman!

MADAM KOFO: Hnm...Funny smell...*(Standing and sniffing all around.)*

DUPE: *(Holding her down.)* Mother! Relax. Let's talk.

MADAM KOFO: Funny. Can't you smell it?

DUPE: What is it like, exactly?

MADAM KOFO: Smoke. Cigarette. Or alcohol. I don't know.

DUPE: *(Pulling her towards the stairs.)* Mommy, I know you're tired. Go to bed.

MADAM KOFO: *(Still sniffing and groping.)* God knows I am. Can't you smell...?

DUPE: *(Dragging her toward the stairs.)* Not a thing, Mommy. Just sleep. *(They hear sounds of the rooster crowing.)*

MADAM KOFO: *(Rising, stretching and stepping up.)* I hear you. Time to sleep. But I need to find...*(She turns and quickly steps down, heading for the closet. But DUPE is still trying to pull her away. Taking off her wig.)* Child, leave me alone. I must take off...

DUPE: *(Hurriedly.)* You will. I'll take your wig. Sleep, Mommy.

MADAM KOFO: But I will, soon. Now let me rest. *(Pause, listens.)* But this...It's so...so stuffy. Can't breathe. *(She leans forward and tries to crack the window open. But DUPE is already ahead of her.)*

DUPE: Mommy, I will...*(Dropping her mother's hand, she hurries to the window. Now free, MADAM KOFO wanders off to the closet, hears the snoring and opens the closet.)*

MADAM KOFO: *(Alarmed.)* What is this? *(Screams.)* Dupe! *(Startled, PRINCE is half-awake.)*

PRINCE: *(Groggily.)* What...What's...your problem, woman? *(MADAM KOFO gives him a loud clap on his face. Finally, PRINCE gets his rude awakening.)* Hell. What's...going on here? You talking me...for a ride?

MADAM KOFO: *(Incensed.)* You'll soon find out. *(She makes to slap him again, but DUPE intercepts her.)*

DUPE: Stop!

MADAM KOFO: Don't you touch me, you "b..."

DUPE: Please...Please Mommy...*(They struggle.)*

MADAM KOFO: *(Holding PRINCE's collar.)* Don't you dare

please me now! Out! Go please yourself. *(Awkward silence as DUPE steps aside.)* No wonder! So this is what you have been doing in my absence? And in my house? Pros...sl...? *(She slaps DUPE.)*

DUPE: *(Screaming.)* My Galahad! *(As the struggle continues, SHAKARA crosses to the garage door in readiness for her escape, but finds no exit. The door is locked. In desperation, she makes her way towards the front door, only to come face-to-face with MADAM KOFO who blocks her way with her body.)*

MADAM KOFO: *(Pursuing SHAKARA.)* And more? *(The struggle intensifies. MADAM KOFO is still holding onto PRINCE's collar as she tries to stop SHAKARA. PRINCE too is struggling as he's choking. In the melee, SHAKARA finally pushes her way through and runs towards the gate. But THE GUARD/ALAWO has locked the gate. She tries to fly over, but stumbles and falls. MADAM KOFO's shoes are now flying up in the air as she runs after her. Finally, she's caught up with SHAKARA and pins her down. Caught in a dead-end, SHAKARA groans. In the pandemonium that ensues, DUPE tries to let PRINCE out, but fails. PRINCE is rather amused by it all. Outside, from the neighborhood, a familiar tune "Blood, Blood, Blood and Fire" is playing.)*

DUPE: *(Struggling with her mother.)* My friends, please! Please, Mommy!

MADAM KOFO: *(Pushing her away.)* Friend? Indeed! Out! Out of my sight! You piglet! *(Beating SHAKARA.)* Caught! Yes! God catch you! Judgment! *(Frantic.)* Alawo! Don't open the gate!

DUPE: She's my friend. Mommy, how can you be so cruel?

MADAM KOFO: One can only be accused of being cruel to somebody. Not this...No! Nobody!

DUPE: Pleeeaaase stop! *(But her mother will not listen, and kicks DUPE out.)*

MADAM KOFO: Go away, you traitor! I will never trust you again. Not in this life! I'm calling the police!

DUPE: *(Loud echo.)* Mommy pleaseeeeeeese! For my sake! For her mother's sake. It's mother's...I mean nanny Omesiete's daughter. Remember? For her sake...

MADAM KOFO: All the more reason why she must suffer for this. Ha! Ha! Ha! We'll see who laughs last! *(She turns to dial the phone.)*

DUPE: *(Trailing her, crying out loud.)* Don't call the police, Mommy. Please! Please! Please! Mommy, pleaseeeeeeeeese!

MADAM KOFO: I say over my dead body! You'll regret, forever! *(Struggling to pull the phone cord with her toes.)*

DUPE: *(Exploding.)* Then so be it! Witch! You'll get your reward. Soon! You think you'll hurt me like this and go free? Never! I'm ready for you!

MADAM KOFO: Yes, go ahead! Slut! Shame on you if you don't!

DUPE: *(Yelling.)* Witch! Iya-Ajee! Won't you let me have my peace? All my life, you have brought me nothing but pain. I have no mother. I have no father. You don't love me. Only your money. And the ones that love me, you hurt and don't want to see. You'll pay dearly for this! I'm leaving. *(DUPE rushes into the house to start packing. Door opens. Outside, the music gets louder and louder: "Blood, Blood, Blood and Fire. Judgment has come and mercy has gone.")*

MADAM KOFO: *(Screaming.)* Go! Fast! Shame on you if you ever come back to me! *(She grabs SHAKARA's arm.)*

SHAKARA: *(Terrified.)* Please. Please Ma!

MADAM KOFO: Robber! Olee! Shut up! *(Calling to THE GUARD/ALAWO.)* Police! Guard! Call the police! *(But THE GUARD/ALAWO is nowhere to be found.)* Where is that idiot? Alawo! *(MADAM KOFO strains to press a button. SHAKARA quickly pulls herself back and escapes. Sirens sound as the police arrive. THE GUARD/ALAWO has changed into the POLICE OFFICER ONE.)*

POLICE OFFICER ONE: You called, Madam?

MADAM KOFO: Yes. These robbers attacked me...my estate. Arrest them. *The POLICE OFFICER ONE grabs the male suspect and puts handcuffs around his wrists. MADAM KOFO notices that SHAKARA is not there.)* Where? Where is she? *(Yelling.)* She's gone? That thief! Wait! I'll get her too.

POLICE OFFICER ONE: Who?

MADAM KOFO: *(Panting.)* The other one! The girl robber. *(She storms into the house. Returns quickly.)* She's gone! Don't worry, I'll get her! *(PRINCE looks unruffled. The POLICE OFFICER ONE starts to interrogate the male suspect.)*

POLICE OFFICER ONE: Your name?

PRINCE: *(Haughtily leaning on the gate.)* Prince.

POLICE OFFICER ONE: *(With authority.)* Now attention! Do you know you're talking to a police officer?

MADAM KOFO: *(Shutting the front door.)* Yes, good. Thieves only hear with a rude hand! He wants to spoil my innocent child. Yes. Teach him a lesson! *(POLICE OFFICER ONE kicks PRINCE as he barks.)* Criminals!

POLICE OFFICER ONE: Young. Very young.

MADAM KOFO: They're dangerous. All of them. *(PRINCE smiles, stands defiant.)*

POLICE OFFICER ONE: *(Stunned.)* Are you mad? *(In anger, he knocks off the spectacles from PRINCE's face. PRINCE smiles, tries to pick them up, but he fails.)*

PRINCE: Officer, you must be hungry. *(He tries to reach into his pocket, but can't. He throws down his wallet.)* I got cash.

POLICE OFFICER ONE: *(Giving him a glare.)* Are you mad?

PRINCE: *(Smiling.)* That helps, too.

POLICE OFFICER ONE: *(Shaking his head.)* You see? That's what we're faced with today. I mean, every day. Defiant, fearless, shameless, young criminals. Obstructing a police officer? You'll see. *(He starts writing furiously in his log book.)* What is your name?

PRINCE: *(Haughtily.)* Prince.

POLICE OFFICER ONE: *(Still writing.)* Prince of Thieves! Prince what?

PRINCE: Justice.

POLICE OFFICER ONE: *(Mocking.)* Ha! Justice my foot! *(Thinking.)* Your blasted name?

PRINCE: Prince Justice.

POLICE OFFICER ONE: *(Writing.)* Huh? *(Suddenly realizes, startled.)* Did you say Prince Justice?

PRINCE: Yes.

POLICE OFFICER ONE: *(Alarmed.)* Ah, my Gaaaaad! That's the thief...I mean... chief...son of the b... Our boss! God! You're only the son of my Chief?

PRINCE: *(Smiling.)* I told you so. *(In a mad rush, the POLICE OFFICER ONE takes off PRINCE's handcuffs.)*

POLICE OFFICER ONE: *(Fretting.)* Ha...An accident of...sight. Sorry sir. *(Smiling nervously.)* Ehnm...This didn't happen. Ehm...your father, you know. This is not good for his ears...I mean, nerves. Please, keep it confidential. Completely to yourself. It just didn't happen! *(Sees MADAM KOFO returning to the scene.)* Mistaken identity, Madam!

MADAM KOFO: *(Annoyed.)* What the hell is wrong with you, Officer? Don't waste my bloody time, o'jare! What are you waiting for? Take the stinking criminal out of my premises. And lock him up!

POLICE OFFICER ONE: *(Fidgeting.)* Madam, make...ehm... Make dis one...I mean, Madam. If na de girl? Okay. But dis one, can't. I can't take de boy. Where is the partner? I mean the girl. That one we can take.

MADAM KOFO: What?

POLICE OFFICER ONE: Too many men in the cell. No women. We need...we're searching...*(Now, the SHOWBOY TWO has arrived on the scene as a backup POLICE MAN TWO. The former turns to his colleague.)* Not so?

POLICE MAN TWO: Na true, Sergeant. Plenty men for

(h)inside jail. But women scarce like money.

MADAM KOFO: What nonsense? Act...action!

POLICE OFFICER ONE: *(Taking a deep breath.)* Madam, the long and short of de tin is dis. Dat one na...we Oga pickin.

MADAM KOFO: What nonsense?

POLICE OFFICER ONE: Our Chief's son? You wan make I lose my job? Otio! No!

MADAM KOFO: Criminals?

POLICE MAN TWO: That's how they all are. The snake can only give birth to a long thing. Not so, Madam? *(Trying to soothe her.)* Ha! Haba, Madam! You wan pour sand-sand for my garri? *(Raising his right arm.)* See me-o, Madam. Notin dey for my *(h)*arm-pit! I no fit. I no fit lose my job for nobody.

MADAM KOFO: *(Stunned.)* Whaaaaat? You rotten police!

POLICE OFFICER ONE: No, Madam. We're not rotten. It's the law! Ha! Ha! Ha!

MADAM KOFO: The law? Nonsense! What's this country coming to? You'll see! All of you. I'm going to teach you all a lesson. I'm seeing the DPO Commissioner. And I'll press charges. Get ready! Now! *(Vexed, she runs back in to get ready.)*

POLICE MAN TWO: *(Giggling.)* Yeye woman. Run to hell...to hellele! God's case?

POLICE OFFICER ONE: No appear! Ha! Ha! Ha! *(He turns to PRINCE.)* Old boy, go home. Return to sender. Salute your Papa. Great man! He keeps us in good business! Ha! Ha! Ha! *(POLICE OFFICER ONE turns to POLICE MAN TWO and gives his order.)* Corporal, take the young Chief home. And make sure he's safe!

POLICE MAN ONE: *(Military salute.)* Yes, sergeant! We'll take him to daddy! *(PRINCE smiles, turns to POLICE OFFICER ONE. PRINCE is completely free. POLICE MAN TWO escorts PRINCE home.)*

MADAM KOFO: *(Returning.)* So you're letting him go? The

thief? Rapist who dares to violate my innocent child? Eh? Is that fair?

POLICE OFFICER ONE: *(Smiling.)* Madam. What is fair in this land of ours?

MADAM KOFO: Nothing.

POLICE OFFICER ONE: Only Law enforcement.

MADAM KOFO: *(Angrily.)* Rotten! Dead!

POLICE OFFICER ONE: *(Smiling.)* Easy Madam! Let go!

MADAM KOFO: Can't you hear? I say over my dead body! I'm done. Done with this nonsense forever. No! I won't take it anymore. Neither in this life nor in the next. Everything is going to end right here. Now!

POLICE OFFICER ONE: No use, Madam. Save your breath. Save time. Save money. Rest, Madam. Peace. *(Departing, POLICE OFFICER ONE is so amused, he starts whistling "Time na money-o! Oli-nan-do! Time na money. Oli-nan-do. Made you use your time well. Olinando. No spoil another man..." Laughs.)* Dat na we country. Case closed! *(The door slams. Exit POLICE OFFICER ONE. Outside, the Police van is heard hitting the tarmac.)*

MADAM KOFO: *(Alone, sighs.)* Why does anyone bother with bastards? *(Turning to go inside.)* My business is with my daughter. Deaf as she is, she's going to hear me by force. You people are going to see. It's either me or her. Today! *(She goes to confront her daughter at the front door. Another cock crow. It's daybreak now. Voices outside.)* So this is what you do with my house in my absence? Ehn?

DUPE: But...Mom...

MADAM KOFO: Don't 'Mom' me. Ever!

DUPE: *(Cajoling.)* Mooommmy, listen! Listen to me for once!

MADAM KOFO: Another life. Over. It's over. Leave me alone. Go. I want my peace.

DUPE: You'll have it! Wait...

MADAM KOFO: *(Furiously.)* No! No waiting now! I'm tired.

Tired and tired of struggling and struggling to make something out of you. But this is all I get. Nothing. It's no use. Nothing is. I'm done.

DUPE: But Mommy, you're making such a big deal out of nothing.

MADAM KOFO: Yes, that's what you are. Nothing. What you've made out of yourself. Frolicking with skunks.

DUPE: But Mommy. It's not like she's a complete stranger. You know her...

MADAM KOFO: I don't! Don't want to know nobody!

DUPE: Mommy, but we grew up together. She and I...

MADAM KOFO: God forbid that my own blood should grow up with such wretches!

DUPE: It doesn't matter. We're friends.

MADAM KOFO: Friends, my foot! *(Pause.)* Whoever told you that you were friends? The Prince I can understand. But that other one?

DUPE: Mommy, she's my best...my very best friend...family...

MADAM KOFO: Don't you ever soil your heritage by messing around scums. You hear me? I'm your mother. For nine whole months, I carried you. Labored, hard. Wiped your running nose. Cleaned up your stinking ar...*(Voice cracking, pause.)* And...and...and...now. *(Pause.)* This is all I get. You? My own daughter? Telling me you're family with...with scums and...Ah life! *(Sighing.)* No use. Go with them. Your new family. I can't help you. With or without you, I'm moving on. Done! Gone! And nothing is going to stop me. Out! Out of my sight. Out of my life! You deaf one. You'll never understand. *(She steps into the front door, picks up a broom and starts sweeping furiously. DUPE tries to brush off the dust that's falling all over her.)*

DUPE: *(Irritated as more dirt descends on her.)* No, Mommy, I don't. I don't understand. And never will. What's wrong with a young girl being friends with another girl?

MADAM KOFO: Many things are wrong "Miss so...so...So-cialist!" Abi! Yes, there's everything wrong with that in the world. You hear me? Yes. Everything is wrong when every Tom, Dick and Harry can come carrying their lice infested heads into my house! And I must be silent when the bags of trash are falling over my precious... seed. Ehn?

DUPE: Yes. That's all you know. That's all we hear. Your precious weed. Treasured stench!

MADAM KOFO: Is this what I get for all that I've done?

DUPE: What on earth have you done?

MADAM KOFO: What on earth haven't I done? I've been your savior!

DUPE: Yeah, right! Did you ever have time for me? You've always had your weeds. Your nursery. You nursed them; not me. That was more important. And still you want to deny me the right to my aloneness? Oh! Tyranny! Won't you let me be? Let me be? Alone! Seek my own company! *(Loudly.)* I'm sick and tired! Tired! Tired of living in this mess! I'm through! And through! *(DUPE storms out noisily into her room and reemerges with her brief case, a pair of shoes dangling on her shoulder, a towel, and a belt on her elbow. Her mother tries to block her way, but DUPE is determined. She heads for the gate. MADAM KOFO follows, trying to pull her down as DUPE is now leaping high up on the gate. The struggle continues between mother and daughter. Finally, DUPE overpowers her mother and leaps forward to jump across but her dress gets caught in it.)*

MADAM KOFO: *(Alarmed.)* Duuuuuuupe! *(No response.)* Dupe! Stop! *(Silence as DUPE continues struggling. Frantically the mother calls.)* Help! Help! My daughter! That girl will be my death!

DUPE: *(Still hanging, panting.)* You know it. Get ready!

MADAM KOFO: *(Alarmed and wailing.)* Mo kwu! I'm dead-O! What's come over my child? Ehn? Where do I go from here? Where did I go wrong?

DUPE: *(Trying to break free.)* Everywhere! Everything! Search. Search your soul.

MADAM KOFO: I'm innocent. I've done nothing.

DUPE: *(Kicking from the wall.)* That's precisely the problem! You've done nothing. "Misses Innocent!" Nothing for me. Or for anybody except your bloated ego...image. And...that's why we're all in this mess.

MADAM KOFO: Shut up!

DUPE: No, you can't shut me up!

MADAM KOFO: So this is the abuse I get after all I've done for you? Eh?

DUPE: You've given me nothing but pain. Pain. Do I have a mother or father? In my entire life, you've held me in this orphanage called home. No, all that you used to tie me up and manipulate me must...must...must...*(She starts choking, breaks the gold necklace around her neck and throws it at her mother before landing hard on the ground.)* That's the best you've given me. Take. Take it. I'm done.

MADAM KOFO: Breaking off the gold chain I gave you for your birthday?

DUPE: Yes. I want no memories of you. No ties.

MADAM KOFO: Ingrate. Do you know the cost?

DUPE: I don't know and I don't care. Go hug your jewelry.

MADAM KOFO: To get this from my own child? No respect? I can't take this anymore. *(Tries to slap DUPE, but the child ducks.)*

DUPE: *(Defiant.)* Go ahead and do your worse. But you can't shut me up. No. Not any more. I've stewed in silence all my life.

MADAM KOFO: What? Do I hear right?

DUPE: Yes. Right! For seventeen years, you've cooked me in silence. Now the lid is off. Ready to blast...

MADAM KOFO: Help. Heeeeelp meeeee! My baby. *(Trying desperately to pull DUPE back into the yard, but DUPE resists and leaps back, high up onto the gate, so that MADAM KOFO cannot reach her.)*

DUPE: *(Kicking, struggling.)* I'm no baby! And that's your problem. Stop treating me like a child. I'm a young adult. Some of my mates are now married with children. *(Meanwhile, VOICES of the community led by SHOWBOY ONE and TWO intervene outside.)*

VOICES: What is wrong? What is the matter? Neighbor?

MADAM KOFO: My Angel. Going...

DUPE: No. Not yours. Go Satan! And leave me alone.

VOICES: Come, lady! Come down.

DUPE: No!

VOICES: Down. Nothing gets settled by running or escaping it. Hold! *(With her mother pulling from inside, hands are seen pulling DUPE down from the street side of the gate.)*

DUPE: No! Let me gooooooo! *(DUPE's strained voice rocks the entire neighborhood.)*

MADAM KOFO: *(Frantically.)* Help! She won't hear me. *(Wailing.)* Gooood! Who's bewitching my daughter? Where do I go? What am I to do? Please, someone. Alawo, go call me the Chairman! No, Shanka the DPO! Oh, my God! Chief! Where are you all now? I need you. My only child. My only hope. God, where are you?

DUPE: Yeah, right! It's now you know? *(The struggle intensifies, with the VOICES of the community intervening. MADAM KOFO falls, rises. With their hands assisting her from the other side of the gate, they push DUPE back into her mother's hands. DUPE resists and lands hard on the ground and limps as she clutches on to her bruised knee. Silence, as DUPE bleeds and nurses her wounds. Somewhat relieved, but still panting, MADAM KOFO moves to examine DUPE's body for injuries.)*

MADAM KOFO: Are you hurt, my Angel?

DUPE: *(Spitefully.)* Yes. You hurt me. *(MADAM KOFO bends over to examine the gaping wound, but DUPE rebuffs her, groaning.)* See? I'm wounded.

MADAM KOFO: Me too. I'm injured.

DUPE: By whom?

MADAM KOFO: *(Hesitating.)* Somebody...everybody. *(Silence.)* Hnm...child. Someday, you, too, will know...*(She cautions herself.)* It's not my fault.

DUPE: Whose?

MADAM KOFO: I didn't mean to.

DUPE: You've never meant anything.

MADAM KOFO: *(Bending.)* Let me...

DUPE: Don't touch me! *(MADAM KOFO realizes that the VOICES of the neighbors are still lingering. She waves them off.)*

MADAM KOFO: Thanks for helping. *(Pause.)* And please leave us alone. It's our family business. We all have our share. I'll sort things out with my daughter. *(Voices disappear. Silence.)* But Dupe! Dupe! What have I done?

DUPE: What have you not done?

MADAM KOFO: My dear. What? After all my sacrifice?

DUPE: Your ritual sacrifice. No thanks. Not for me. Keep that for the vultures that you...

MADAM KOFO: Me? Vultures?

DUPE: Yes!

MADAM KOFO: *(Hysterical.)* Ehn? God? What is this? What is going on? Is this the end? *(DUPE continues resisting and pulling away from her as the mother desperately tries to woo her back.)*

DUPE: *(Spitefully.)* Your end!

MADAM KOFO: Ah no! God forbid! *(Pause.)* My Angel! My love!

DUPE: Yeah, right! Don't touch me with your bloody hands! Don't! Get it? I'm nothing! Nothing! Leave me alone!

MADAM KOFO: So you really mean it? You want to run away? Eh? *(Stretching to embrace DUPE.)* Come, my love.

DUPE: I'm not. Go to your lovers.

MADAM KOFO: Aye miii—O! So my child's gone? I've lost my daughter? Ehn?

DUPE: Leave me! It's now you know that I'm your daughter. I've been your prisoner.

MADAM KOFO: No darling. I was only trying to protect you.

DUPE: Protect who? Me? From you or...?

MADAM KOFO: Stop talking nonsense, child! I'm your mother. I have an obligation to guard...I mean guide...

DUPE: Right! Guard your prisoner. Can't you see it's over? I'm going. *(Storming out, but her mother continues to pull her back.)* Leave me alone! After all, I'm used to being alone. You've never been there for me. And the friends I make, you never want to set eyes on them. Don't you choose your own friends? Why? Why? Why must I die in your jail forever? All I want is the freedom to have friends. Madam dic...dictator...Is that criminal?

MADAM KOFO: Don't be ridiculous, Dupe! The question is not whether or not you should have friends, but what kind of friends you choose. Understand?

DUPE: No!

MADAM KOFO: Darling, listen to me. As a parent, and a single parent for that matter, I'm concerned...I should... Ensure that my daughter chooses the proper people.

DUPE: Ha! Ha! Ha! *Proper people,* indeed! It would be quite interesting to know who "your" proper people are.

MADAM KOFO: And that's where your parents must come in. Because you're still young and cannot tell your right from your left.

DUPE: I'm not a child anymore! Hear? I'm seventeen. Understand? And don't you ever make that mistake again. That's what you parents do. Always underestimating your children. Always overprotecting. Always assuming that teenagers are irresponsible and helpless. That you must have to do, and decide, everything for them. *(Emphatically.)* Especially when they are girls. I'm sick and tired of being underrated and told what to do.

MADAM KOFO: Then what are parents for, if not to give guidance to their own children? And girls? *(Cajoling.)* Listen, darling. Girls are much more vulnerable. And that is why they must be guarded...Oh damn the guard. Guided!

DUPE: *(Mock laughter.)* I see. Girls are prisoners. See? That's what...

MADAM KOFO: No child!

DUPE: I'm no child. So don't...okay?

MADAM KOFO: *(Tries a military salute.)* I hear you, "General D." But you see, I'm only trying to do my duty as a parent, to keep the tradition.

DUPE: Yeah! Tradition! That is why we cannot move forward in this country, because the old live in the past. Fixed on it. They hate change. They must see everything done the way they themselves did it in their own time. Music cannot change because parents danced to folk music in their own time. Rap music, rock 'n roll and everything youths love is, to them, nothing but noise! Noise! *(Stunned, MADAM KOFO watches her, silently.)* But I tell you parents, your generation is wrong. Crippled. Deaf. Dumb. And blind. Yes, that is why we're in this mess. So don't blame the kids. Blame yourselves— Parents! *(Pause.)* Now, if you're my mother, who's my father? Or don't I deserve to know? At seventeen? I'm still not old enough to know? Ehn, Mother-Rich? *(Choking.)* Ah...ah...you...you're unfair. So unfair! *(Silence.)* If you say that your children are wrong...something has gone wrong with a whole generation. Who is responsible? Who made it that way? Who raised the children to be wrong? Hey, Mother, don't let me tell you! For if you're really honest enough to admit it, you're part of the crisis and chaos. Yes! That's the truth! Just because you have money? You think you can use your blood money to tyrannize everybody. Huh? Just wait. It won't be long now. You're going to pay. You will pay! And dearly too. Take it from me! You, maker of the stinking mess!

MADAM KOFO: Yes, I hear you, "B...Goddess!"

DUPE: Right. Your last chance to search...your dying soul.

MADAM KOFO: *(Laughing listlessly.)* Yes, god...dess. *(Suddenly, exploding.)* Shut up!

DUPE: No, you can't shut me up! Not any more!

MADAM KOFO: *(Vexed.)* Alawo, where are you? *(DUPE is hysterical, her loud voice competing with her mother's.)*

THE GUARD/ALAWO: *(Approaching nervously.)* Mo...

MADAM KOFO: Alawo, go immediately and call me Uncle Shanka, the DPO.

THE GUARD/ALAWO: *(Hesitating.)* Mo?

MADAM KOFO: Don't 'Moo' me, cow! Run! Or what's the matter with you? You're deaf?

THE GUARD/ALAWO: Otio! No Mo. But...

MADAM KOFO: *(Giving him a whack on the head.)* But what? Carry your dead body out! Out! Imbecile! *(Wagging her finger at DUPE.)* You'll see! I'll show you! *(Grabs the phone and dials furiously.)* Hello! Yes, the Chairman. *(Digging deep with her big toe.)* Ahn. You're there! Yes, my love. It's urgent. Very urgent. Come. No. Now. I want you...I need you. Chief, pleeease. Now! No. Not our precious weeds. Just this unruly girl. Yes, Dupe. Completely out of control now. Just like a rabid dog. Bitch. Can't stand it anymore. Yes, come! *(While she's on the phone, DUPE is fuming.)*

DUPE: Call me whatever ugly name you like. It won't bother me. Nothing. I know who I am. Not what anybody calls or says I am. Ha! Ha! Ha! *(Pause.)* So I'm now the bitch? Hooray! I made it to the Honor Roll of Bitches. Your Baby-Bitch! Eh, Madam Kofo? I'm now a bitch because I have...one boyfriend. Is it a crime?

MADAM KOFO: Yes!

DUPE: Then let be. *(Pause.)* And by the way, who taught me? Not you, my great teacher? *(Silence.)* Ah, if only you knew just how much I've learnt from you? Not to be like you? Ha! It's no use. This mess. I've learnt one good lesson from life: "You don't need a mother to be born!"

MADAM KOFO: *(Aims for DUPE, but she ducks.)* How dare you? You brat! You owe your life to the stinking mess. Without my stinking mess, you'd be nothing. Have nothing!

DUPE: *(Yelling.)* And you think I care? You're wrong. Very wrong! And listen to me. Now. You cannot gag me! Do your worst, wicked woman. Do your worst! Your own reward is coming! Yes! Get ready! *(She storms out again with her suitcase.)*

MADAM KOFO: *(Running after her, pleading.)* Dupe! Dupe! Come back!

DUPE: You're wasting your time. I'm done. I'm out of here.

MADAM KOFO: *(Wailing.)* Aye meee-O! Come see me see trouble-O! Security! Security-Guard! Me-Guard! Alawo! Where are you?

THE GUARD/ALAWO: *(Breathless.)* Here!

MADAM KOFO: You too? Traitor? Where have you been. *(Aiming to slap him. ALAWO ducks, her arm hits the wall.)*

THE GUARD/ALAWO: You sent me...

MADAM KOFO: Where? Liar! *(Groaning.)* It's over. My arms broken. These witches are going to kill me.

THE GUARD/ALAWO: *(Aside.)* Nobody else is killing you but yourself.

MADAM KOFO: What? Alawo? You too? What did you say?

THE GUARD/ALAWO: Ahh, notin. Notin at all-at all. I just dey pray for you. *(Swearing under his breath.)* Make you suffer too! Your dead soul. God take am.

MADAM KOFO: *(Groaning.)* Amen, my faithful. God hear your prayer. *(Still groaning, she closes her eyes in prayer.)* Alawo, pray. Pray for me.

THE GUARD/ALAWO: *(Eyes shut.)* Yes, Mo. I dey pray. Very-very hard. God go pay you back for everytin you done do. E no deaf. God pays us all. E dey hear me.

MADAM KOFO: Amen. God hears you, my faithful. Don't stop. Continue. Forgive. I trust...God will hear you, I know. *(She groans.)*

THE GUARD/ALAWO: True. True, Madam!

MADAM KOFO: My God! God, what have I done? God help me! I'm lost! I'm gone! *(DUPE rushes back, slamming the gate behind her. Her mother seizes her, panting.)* Ama...Alawo! I need you. The key. The gate! My daughter. Don't! Don't...(She chokes.)*

THE GUARD/ALAWO: Yes, Mo. De key dey here. You too "rocky." *(MADAM KOFO struggles with her daughter by the gate.)*

MADAM KOFO: *(Choking.)* Lucky? Hnm...me? *(She's choking.)*

THE GUARD/ALAWO: *(Opening the gate.)* Rock. Yes, Madam. You get rock. Plenty rock, Maa.

MADAM KOFO: *(Screaming.)* Which luck? Fool! Lock the gate I say! *(Too late. DUPE has escaped through the gate. Her mother follows.)* Come, people. Hold. Hold her. Someone has bewitched my only child. The evil ones have done their worst. I must go see the native doctor! They've put a curse on her...My Angel...!

DUPE: *(Fleeing.)* You, my Mother, are the curse on me.

MADAM KOFO: Me? How?

DUPE: Your heartless...Your stinking money. That's the curse! *(Screaming. Her mother intercepts her.)* Somebody save me! Save me from my mother!

MADAM KOFO: Help me! Help me! Save my daughter!

DUPE: Save me!

MADAM KOFO: Help me! Help me! My daughter! Neighbor! *(She sees the DPO/SHANKA and runs to him.)* Shanka! God! Our father. Where? Where are you? Come! Save!

114

You alone can save...Oh Father! Come! She's going! Shanka! Come help me Fatheeeeeeeeeeer!

DPO/SHANKA: *(Alarmed, hurrying to arrest the situation.)* What the hell is going on here? Ehn? *(As the DPO grabs DUPE's left arm, MADAM KOFO holds onto the other. He studies the tense situation, DUPE's face especially, and tries to diffuse the tension.)* Somebody hurt my "Lady D?"

DUPE: *(Sobbing.)* She, alone. Hurting...crushing me. Just tell her to let me be.

MADAM KOFO: *(Trembling.)* Me, hurt you? Dupe, just look at me. It's me, you know? *(Silence.)*

DPO/SHANKA: *(Softly.)* Risi. Calm down. We have her. She's not going. *(He gives her a hug.)*

MADAM KOFO: *(In pain, holding her chest.)* No. But...Oh, Shanka. My heart! My heart! I'm tired! Tired! I'm finished. Help me!

DPO/SHANKA: *(Smiling.)* You know I have, always. From the very beginning, I've always been there. *(He coughs, checks himself. Turns to cuddle DUPE.)* My "Lady D." *(Turns to MADAM KOFO.)* This girl is not as bad as you think, you know. You need to be more careful. More cautious. You can see she's hurting for whatever reason. No amount of force can do it. Learn the art of human management. It's very important. As they say, "You cannot force the milk-teeth." Can you?

MADAM KOFO: I know-I know-I know. Now I don't know if it's been worth it all.

DPO/SHANKA: Stop Risi! Is this you wallowing in self-pity? I've never known you to be that way. *(Pause.)*

MADAM KOFO: That child has tamed me...taught me. I'm no longer the same.

DPO/SHANKA: That's no news! Which parent hasn't been taught?

MADAM KOFO: I said tamed.

DPO/SHANKA: Whatever. Taught or tamed? Same ten and

ten pence. Well, which parents haven't been schooled by their children? Ehn? Tell me? *(Pause.)* My dear, me too. I'm one of you here. I know just what you feel because, in spite of my uniform, I too have been a parent. And I understand. Believe me, I do. Children, teenagers especially, always have a way of challenging, teaching or taming parents. Ask these folks here. They know. *(Turning to the audience.)* People, don't you all have your own stories to tell? *(Pause for reactions.)* Well, you hear them! All of them. Parenting is bringing up, and polishing up, your own from the very raw state of nature. Which for me, is the ultimate challenge. Ask parents!

MADAM KOFO: But none is as difficult as mine.

DPO/SHANKA: Well, who says? How do you know?

MADAM KOFO: I know it. And you, Shanka, you just know how it's been from the very start. Or you've forgotten?

DPO/SHANKA: How can I? I still remember.

MADAM KOFO: Every bit of that agonizing scene. When I found me. And you, Shanka, were my savior then. Now save me. Save me for this last time. 'Cause I'm finished. You made a promise, remember?

DPO/SHANKA: Yes, I did. I will always keep my own part of the bargain, so long as you keep yours. Stay on the side of the law, always. That's all I ask. And that's only fair. *(Turning to the audience.)* Is it news what I'm saying that teenagers challenge their parents? So, now tell me, what's wrong? What do you want me to do?

MADAM KOFO: *(Agonizing.)* Beyond me. Beyond control. Ah, my own child. Challenging my authority? No, I can't. Can't anymore. I've done my very best. No more. I cannot cope. Take her...she's in your hands.

DPO/SHANKA: *(Laughing.)* Is that all? You're giving up? Oh, teenagers and parents! And tell me just what you want me to do this time.

MADAM KOFO: *(Wailing.)* Ayee mee-o! My life! Not...nothing...

DPO/SHANKA: 'Nothing?' And you invite me here with this noisy palava? Ah, Risi! Come out with it, for once!

MADAM KOFO: It's nothing. Just this daughter, Dupe... getting out of control. She won't hear me...listen to anything I say. You already know my story with this child.

DPO/SHANKA: I know.

MADAM KOFO: She says she's now a teenager. She's grown up and won't listen.

DPO/SHANKA: Is it news that teenager don't listen? Today's teenagers? Ugh! *(Sighs and takes a deep breath.)* My Risi, come make I ask. You dey for dis contry at all? *(Stroking DUPE, who's still trying to pull away from his strong hold.)* Risi, re-lax. God don butter your bread. No worry. Everything dey ok. No worry. Me, I go take charge. I'm fully in control. Now!

MADAM KOFO: Amiiii-O! Amen! God will bless you, as you, my friend, have come to rescue me. I beg, save me from me...I mean, from this mess.

DPO/SHANKA: I'm ready. Don't worry. I've told you, I'm taking charge. And we're going to triumph. So, rest. Make you lie cooleee. Peace. Leave de matter to me.

MADAM KOFO: *(Relieved.)* What are you going to do?

DPO/SHANKA: I go talk to am. You see, experience they say, is the best teacher. This job has taught me to talk to people to create understanding. Even children nowadays, you need to understand them so you can handle them with better care. Make them friends. Children do make wonderful friends. Once you've won them over, you can eat from their hands. Even the most stubborn ones. *(Turning to DUPE.)* My lady, take it easy with your mother. At times, parents go wrong. We have faults. She does...I mean...but ehm...*(Takes DUPE's hands.)* Don't worry. Whatever your problem, we'll take care. Meanwhile, "Lady D," go take a warm bath. Very good for bruised nerves. And see me later if you wish. *(Exit DUPE. The DPO turns to go.)*

MADAM KOFO: *(Excitedly.)* Wait, my dear. I just got an idea.

DPO/SHANKA: What? Tell me.

MADAM KOFO: Hnm...that girl...her so-called friend. I'm going to bring her. Use her...

DPO/SHANKA: What? How?

MADAM KOFO: *(Excitedly.)* I know. I know. I got it. Got her. Oh, Shanka! I've found it!

DPO/SHANKA: What are you talking about? Say it!

MADAM KOFO: *(Mumbling.)* I can't. Not now. Until the time comes...*(Hugging him.)* Oh God, my God! Everything's coming together.

DPO/SHANKA: *(Rising.)* Well, good luck! I must be going.

MADAM KOFO: Thank you so much for always being there. When do I expect to see you again?

DPO/SHANKA: *(At the door.)* Soon. Very soon. Duty calls now. I have to go see the new Police Commissioner.

MADAM KOFO: Tough man, I hear.

DPO/SHANKA: Never takes a 'No' for an answer. His appointment really tells me that our government is ready to fight and win the battle against corruption and drugs.

MADAM KOFO: Those bastards! Messing up people's life and business! If they mess with me, I'll mess with them! Thank goodness. The ex-commissioner of police is still my bosom friend! Just let them try me. I'll show them!

DPO/SHANKA: That's between you and the Law. You're completely on your own. *(Winking at her.)* Catch you later. Goodbye! (Exit DPO/SHANKA. MADAM KOFO is now alone. She's so happy, she starts to pile up bags in one corner. She opens a bag, blesses her precious weed, sniffs into the bag and then takes some quick fox-trot dance steps as she chants "Omesiete-Tomorrow! Tomorrow! Tomorrow! I'll see her tomorrow. That is mine, tomorrow!" For a while, DUPE has re-entered the scene and is watching her, but MADAM KOFO is completely* *unaware of her presence as she darts here and there, kissing one bag after another. DUPE spits out in disgust, and rushes out again as her mother breaks into her victory song.)*

MADAM KOFO: *(Singing.)*

Beta-O!
Na God dey do me beta
Beta-O!
Na God dey do me beta
Katakata don commot
Wahala don commot
No be me dey do-am-O
Na God dey do me beta!

MADAM KOFO: *(Calling.)* Dupe! Dupe! Dupe! *(No answer.)* Well, who knows where she's gone again? Oh well... *(She kisses another bag of drugs, then lifts DUPE's photo.)* Oh, my dear Angel! I love you, very much. And that is why I'm so worried about you. Soon...someday you, too, will understand and forgive my sins. *(Kissing the photo.)* Dupe, my dear! For you...always for you. In your hands...all...Tomorrow, I'll go see that girl's mother. As they say, everything happens for a reason. Who would have known? And all this time, I've been wringing my hands. Tearing hairs over this courier service? And with this new consignment? Ah, God be praised! My bread is buttered over. Tomorrow, I'll put things in her hands. Then it will be over. All this will end tomorrow. *(Exit MADAM KOFO. Light snaps.)*

THE EIGHTH STAGE

The African Sun Has Long Fingernails

(A very warm night. Back in OMESIETE's shack. OMESIE-TE is peeling yams and KECHI is knitting. SHAKARA runs in like a hunted prey.)

SHAKARA: Mother! Mother? *(OMESIETE and KECHI are startled.)*

OMESIETE: What is it?

SHAKARA: Mother!

OMESIETE: Nhnn! Tell now! Who is after you?

SHAKARA: *(Panting.)* Nobody!

OMESIETE: Then why are you running like a refugee? Who's after you?

SHAKARA: *(Breathless.)* The landlady! The landlady! Oh, Mama. I've been...

OMESIETE: *(Supporting her.)* What, child? Talk to me!

SHAKARA: Can't...don't know. I wish...

OMESIETE: *(Frantic. Cuddling her.)* Ebuni! What is the matter with you? Talk to me!

SHAKARA: She's coming. The landlady's coming.

KECHI: To kick us out?

SHAKARA: I don't...But...*(She bends down, picks up a broom.)* Let's just sweep. Clean up the place before she comes. Maybe...maybe it will make her change her mind. *(SHAKARA sweeps the floor with a new burst of energy. OMESIETE and KECHI are dumbfounded and exchange looks. Brief silence, except for SHAKARA's sweeping sounds. Then her mother starts a tune, bends down to continue peeling and slicing her yam chips as KECHI resumes her knitting.)*

OMESIETE: *(Praying.)* Ebuni? You? You too?

KECHI: Mother, you think we're safe?

SHAKARA: Trust me!

KECHI: Me, trust you? That will be the day! Ha!

OMESIETE: *(Smiling.)* Hnm...Who knows? Maybe, at last...Everything is coming together, at last. Hnm...the power of faith. *(Pause.)* You know what "chin-chi" the bedbug told her children?

KECHI: *(Chuckling.)* "Everything hot will get cold."

OMESIETE: You see? Let's wait and see.

KECHI: *(Turning to SHAKARA.)* So, finally? What's come over you?

SHAKARA: Nothing. Just that I'm learning.

KECHI: You? Learning?

OMESIETE: What? From whom?

SHAKARA: *(Pulling KECHI to help with the debris.)* Don't you always talk about faith?

OMESIETE: Yes.

SHAKARA: Then let it be.

KECHI: *(Rocking with laughter.)* Mama, it's time! Get ready to move.

SHAKARA: *(Pulling KECHI.)* Stop that! And come help me to uproot this stump.

KECHI: *(Chuckling, following her.)* Oh yeah! Our tree stump too? Mother, I said it. Something...I just hope we're safe.

OMESIETE: *(Blocking them.)* Please, clean up whatever. But leave my stump alone. It's the only solid place we have to sit on here.

SHAKARA: This place will look better without it. *(She starts shaking up the stump.)*

OMESIETE: *(Stopping her.)* Ebuni? If you break it, where are we going to sit?

SHAKARA: You don't need it. People sit on chairs, not on tree stumps.

121

OMESIETE: *(Gently pushing her away.)* Child, leave my stump alone That's all I have. I can't buy furniture with my eyes, can I? *(SHAKARA gives up on the stump, begins packing up the firewood.)*

SHAKARA: *(Laughing, packing firewood.)* You people self! Don't you know that if we clear up this place, it will look clean and we'll have more space? With that, won't the landlady respect us more? Value us more? I know that woman. *(She yanks the stump and falls flat on her buttocks, but the stump yields. KECHI and OMESIETE laugh, but soon join hands to help her, anyway. Together, they haul the bundle of firewood out of the way and continue to clean up.)*

OMESIETE: So I lived to see this day? So my ancestors have not forgotten me? Ehn?

KECHI: Mama, siddon look.

OMESIETE: Child, tell me. What do you know that I don't?

SHAKARA: Nothing. Just that it's about time...

KECHI: For what?

SHAKARA: To clean up.

KECHI: I can't believe this.

OMESIETE: You? Changed overnight? Child, what do you know that your mother doesn't know?

SHAKARA: A lot Mama. A lot. Oh, mother and sister Kechi! I didn't realize what life could be out there until now. Now I know. I'm ready! *(She embraces them.)*

KECHI: Mama, it's just a spell. I just hope we survive it.

OMESIETE: *(Laughing.)* May the ancestors reward whoever put that spell on you, my daughter! Reward that power for giving me this one chance. Aaaaah ya-ya-yah! *(Taking a few traditional dance steps.)* Omesiete, so you lived to see this day? *(She breaks a piece of kola nut, invokes and offers the pieces to the Earth Goddess. Calling out, as if on a telephone to God.)* God Almighty! So you heard me? At last! *(Singing.)* 'Better-O! Na God dey de me beta!' *(Holding hands together, SHAKARA and*

KECHI join their mother's song. SHAKARA starts drum-
ming with her iron comb on the stump.)

THE FAMILY SONG:

Beta-O!
Na God dey do me beta
Kata don commot
Wahala don commot
No be me dey do-am-O
Na God dey do me beta!

(Suddenly, MADAM KOFO enters. Shocked, OMESIETE
and her daughters are speechless but genuflect to greet
her, anyway. They freeze. Silence.)

MADAM KOFO: *(Smiling.)* You all seem to be doing quite
well.

OMESIETE: *(Stuttering.)* Well...by...God's grace. We'll be...

MADAM KOFO: *(Still smiling.)* True, Omesiete. You and I...I
mean...we need to talk.

OMESIETE: *(Stunned.)* With me?

MADAM KOFO: Yes. As we both know, we've known each
other for a very long time. I think it's time. Time for us
to sort out a few odd things here and there.

OMESIETE: I see. Is it here or should I come with you?

MADAM KOFO: Here. Now. There's no time. The business
cannot wait. It's urgent.

OMESIETE: *(Still stunned.)* Tell me. What is it that cannot
wait? *(MADAM KOFO throws a glance at the girls as a*
sign for them to leave. OMESIETE turns to the girls.) My
babies, please go inside. I'll be with you soon. *(They*
exit, but SHAKARA can be seen peeping from the coco-
nut tree.)

MADAM KOFO: *(Grinning.)* It's nothing much, really. But...
but it's good for you. I mean...I want you or your
younger daughter to join my business.

OMESIETE: Me or my daughter to join you?

MADAM KOFO: Yes.

OMESIETE: Hnm...*(Silence.)* What business now?

MADAM KOFO: Well, I'm just thinking of ways to help you. I know that you people have been living under very difficult conditions. And life is hard and costly nowadays. All I want is just to assist you in any way I can.

OMESIETE: *(Lighting up.)* Oh, my God! Thank God! You alone know just how much help I need.

MADAM KOFO: And I'm here, as they say, "to be the hand of God." To make it happen. For you!

OMESIETE: True?

MADAM KOFO: Yes.

OMESIETE: *(Dancing.)* So this is it? This is that day I have been praying...waiting for? *(She kneels.)* God be praised! So you made me live to see this day? *(Rising.)* Now tell me, God. Speak to me!

MADAM KOFO: It's just a small deal.

OMESIETE: A deal?

MADAM KOFO: A very good deal...for you. For your children. And for mine too. *(Pause, OMESIETE is very attentive.)* I assure you that if you agree to this deal, all your problems will be over.

OMESIETE: *(Excitedly.)* I just can't wait to hear it. Tell me about this business. *(In her corner, SHAKARA is so excited that she resumes her break-dancing. MADAM KOFO pulls OMESIETE to the side. SHAKARA ducks behind, but is still visible to the audience. The women sit on the stump, facing each other.)*

MADAM KOFO: *(Confidentially.)* I have this consignment of eh...eh...Bags...*(Coughs, scratches her head.)* Ehm... bags...you know...All that is needed is just one trip to London.

OMESIETE: *(Rapidly.)* To where? London? Did I hear right?

MADAM KOFO: *(Smiling.)* You are right. Always been right.

And that is why I trust you and yours...Ehm...That is why you have been chosen.

OMESIETE: *(Incredulous.)* Me, chosen? My God! *(Pause.)* So what is involved in this...this...? And my daughter?

MADAM KOFO: Just one trip. One trip and all your problems will be over. *(Confiding in OMESIETE.)* You know, we have a consignment of goods...eh...eh...seed... drugs, you know...Indian Hemp...ehm...some...Co...

OMESIETE: *(Startled.)* Co-what?

MADAM KOFO: *(Cajoling.)* Cocaine, my dear. Nothing wrong with that. Only courage. Calm down.

OMESIETE: *(Thinking.)* Well, Madam. I don't know just how one gets the courage to do...to do these things. *(Pause.)* Tell me, how can anyone be calm with co...caine?

MADAM KOFO: Easy. Very easy. I'll teach. Show you.

OMESIETE: And you want me to...to...?

MADAM KOFO: It doesn't have to be you. In fact, I'd prefer your daughter. Smart girl!

OMESIETE: My daughter?

MADAM KOFO: Your younger daughter. Maybe you don't appreciate. But...I mean...that girl has what it takes. Sharp! A great girl, if you ask me. Just give me your younger daughter. I know she can do it.

OMESIETE: Take my daughter to do what?

MADAM KOFO: A very simple task. Just hop on the plane. Deliver a consignment of the precious seed to my partner in London. He'll be waiting at the airport. Good money. Cool cash! Your family life will never be the same after this. That's how I made it. Many more have, you know. I mean, I rose from down there...Ha! Ha! Ha! And I can show you how.

OMESIETE: And this is what you're asking me...my daughter...Ah ya-ya-yah! *(Pause.)* Why me? Why us?

MADAM KOFO: I told you. You have been chosen. You're a very lucky woman.

OMESIETE: Thank you. I have heard you. *(Silence. Confused, OMESIETE mutters to herself.)* My suffering to end in one day?

MADAM KOFO: Yes. Today! *(Anxious, watching OMESIETE intently.)* Well, tell me. Time is not on my side. What do you say? *(Silence.)* Yes or no? *(OMESIETE is still very deep in thought, muttering to herself.)* Drugs? Jail! Drugs? Jail!

OMESIETE: Ah, Madam. I have heard you. You have done very well. Thank you so very much for thinking of me and my poor children.

MADAM KOFO: *(Excitedly.)* I knew you'd do the right thing. That is why I came. You need it. You're sensible. Wise. You can't stay like this forever. You've always been such a reliable, hardworking woman. How can I continue to watch you suffer like this? No! Believe me, you'll never live to regret this decision.

OMESIETE: I know. *(Resolved with incredible dignity, she rises.)* I hear you. And that is why I say to you Madam. Goodbye!

MADAM KOFO: *(Stunned.)* Good-what?

OMESIETE: Goodbye, Madam. That's all I can say to you now.

MADAM KOFO: What? That's all?

OMESIETE: Goodbye, Madam. And good luck! *(OMESIETE turns to her shanty. MADAM KOFO is so shocked, she sits still on the stump.)*

MADAM KOFO: *(Standing.)* What arrogance?

OMESIETE: *(Walking tall.)* You may use me in any other way, but certainly not in this way Madam. I am poor. I know that I am very, very poor. But Madam, I cannot be anything else but me. Madam, I cannot leave my own dance to dance somebody else's dance. Can't you see?

MADAM KOFO: Enough! You're doomed! And that's why you will die wretched.

OMESIETE: I don't need anybody to tell me where the shoe

pinches me. My pain is my pain. Not anyone else's pain. And I should be the one to complain. Nobody must show me the wound or scar on my body. Because it is me alone who must suffer the pain with my children.

MADAM KOFO: If you do not accept, be ready to move out of this place. Today! Not one more day! Not one more day! Understand?

OMESIETE: (Defiantly.) If that is what it means, Madam, I am ready.

MADAM KOFO: (Hysterical.) Now, pack out! Get ready! Ha! Ha! Ha! The police will soon be here to show you the way out...Out! You stubborn wretched thing!

OMESIETE: (Dignified.) No problem. I'm ready to move. God is my keeper...provider. For everything. I thank God. And for what you too have done, I thank you. Thank you, Madam! (Silence.)

MADAM KOFO: Wretched! Wretched! Forever wretched and backward! Lazy, irresponsible hag! (MADAM KOFO storms out, cursing under her breath. OMESIETE follows. She stands at the border/boundary between the yard and the road, watching her guest leave the premises. Sound of "The Beast" is soon heard hitting the tarmac at high speed. SHAKARA is the first to reemerge from her hideout. She returns briefly to her favorite spot on the stump and starts humming a blues tune. Still alone at the border/edge, OMESIETE's thoughts explode.

OMESIETE: So this is how these people make their money! Ehn? Sick! Sickening disease-money! Me? To have my hand in their rotten business? (Pause.) I know I need the money. Yes. God knows I need money. But I know too the dangers. No! Not this. Certainly not this kind of choking, blood-money. Cocaine? Armed robbery? Indian Hemp? Drugs? Drugs! Quickest way to land in jail. And then what happens? What will happen to my children? And my labor all these years? No! No! These get-rich-quick schemes I know are quite popular nowadays. But...but...My God. If I've waited this long to be...why can't I wait...continue to strive and hope? Someday...

just one day...*(KECHI breaks into her thought.)*

KECHI: So she's gone. What did she say?

OMESIETE: *(Joining her.)* Hnm...my daughter. What can I say? My child. You know that yeye woman?

KECHI: Tell me now!

OMESIETE: Well, call your sister.

KECHI: Ebuni, Ebuni! Mama wants you here. *(SHAKARA simply stares at her sister, then her mother. She sits, humming her blues tune.)*

OMESIETE: *(Taking up SHAKARA's hand.)* Come, my own Ebuni. Don't look so sad.

SHAKARA: Okay, I'm fine. Just leave me alone.

OMESIETE: So, you're not interested to know what the landlady came to say?

SHAKARA: Does it matter? You've made up your mind. And I too have a right to do the same. Don't I?

OMESIETE: Child, you hear her? What do you want me to do or say?

SHAKARA: Many things. But you chose not to.

OMESIETE: Do I have any choice?

SHAKARA: Oh yes, you do! But, as usual, you chose not to. *(Rising.)* That was a lifetime opportunity. Standing right there in front of you. Begging you. But because... because...

KECHI: Somebody tell me! Mama? Ebuni? Tell me. Won't somebody tell me just what in the world is going on here?

SHAKARA: Ask your mother. *(Pause.)* As for me, I thought this was our last chance. I can't help...myself anymore. But for good or bad, something's got to be done. And I'm ready! If I succeed, good. If not, goodbye to you, mother and sister. *(She hurries into the shack, picks up her bad and departs hastily. OMEISETE and KECHI stand and watch helplessly.)*

KECHI: *(Pulling her mother to sit.)* Now you want to cry over spilt milk? *(Silence.)* Leave her. You know how she is. She'll come back again to us when she gets burnt. *(Silence.)* So tell me, what did the landlady say?

OMESIETE: My dear. Taboo. My mouth cannot utter it.

KECHI: What?

OMESIETE: You cannot believe what you are going to hear, my child. The landlady wants me or one of you to join in her drug business.

KECHI: What?

OMESIETE: Yes, my dear. To help deliver some bag of drugs to her partner in London!

KECHI: *(Scornfully.)* Lon-what? Just imagine! That crook!

OMESIETE: See me-o-see trouble-o, my pickin!

KECHI: And of course, you took your stand. Yes! What else is there to it? She can't do anything.

OMESIETE: Except to throw us out of here. Or frame me. Cook up some charges against me, like she's done with others I know who defied her abuse and authority.

KECHI: Nonsense! Just let her try it! Then she'll know that my God, our God does not sleep!

OMESIETE: Yes, my daughter. With God on our side...

KECHI: Who can be against us? *(Pause.)* Mother, you did the right thing to say no. Who wants her blood money to land us in jail?

OMESIETE: Not me.

KECHI: Not me.

OMESIETE: *(Cuddling her.)* Us? Never! *(Pause.)* You remember what my mama said?

KECHI: "Poverty or no poverty..."

KECHI & OMESIETE: *(Together.)* "Nobody can afford to be a plaything."

OMESIETE: Yes! Never let yourself lose your dignity! *(Still holding each other, they sing a song. Light lingers on them for a while until it blossoms into the next scene.)*

THE NINTH STAGE

Fatal Attraction

(MADAM KOFO in her estate. She's darting from here to there. Singing as she cuddles, kisses, and piles up her bags of precious weed one after another when SHAKARA knocks.)

MADAM KOFO: Yes, Alawo. Come in. *(SHAKARA enters, visibly terrified.)*

SHAKARA: *(Courtesies.)* Good day Ma!

MADAM KOFO: *(Realizes who it is, charges at her.)* Yes? What do you want? *(Gives SHAKARA a glare.)*

SHAKARA: *(Stammering.)* Ma...Ma...

MADAM KOFO: *(Bursting into laughter.)* Ahaa! They sent you to find me, eh?

SHAKARA: Nobody. Nobody sent me.

MADAM KOFO: *(Still laughing.)* So they sent you to ruin me and my daughter, eh? Tell them that you didn't find me. Yes! Tell them that you've all failed. *(Suddenly violent.)* Now, get the hell out of my estate, before...*(She calls out.)* Meee-Guard! Alawo!

THE GUARD/ALAWO: *(Standing at attention as he runs in.)* Mo!

MADAM KOFO: Where is my daughter?

THE GUARD/ALAWO: E go out, Mo.

MADAM KOFO: To where?

THE GUARD/ALAWO: I no know, Mo.

MADAM KOFO: Everyone will reap what they sow. Don't worry. You got away before, but not now. Not anymore. Ha! When the police comes, I'll hand you over. Then you'll tell them what you're doing in my estate. *(She presses her security button to alert the police.)* We shall see! We shall see who wins! "She who laughs last, laughs best." Ha! Ha! Ha! *(Suddenly, she stops laughing.)* Alawo, you fed the dog?

THE GUARD/ALAWO: No, Ma.

MADAM KOFO: *(Smiling as she goes to unlock the gate.)* Well, no need. There will be plenty-plenty food *for* the dog...Mince-meat for the Escort. Now! *(Calling the dog.)* Escort! Escort! Attack! *(Dogs barking. SHAKARA is terrified and clings to THE GUARD/ALAWO's waist.)*

SHAKARA: *(Terrified.)* But Ma...Ma...I've come to stay!

MADAM KOFO: With whom? Where?

SHAKARA: With you Ma. I want to be...be with you!

MADAM KOFO: *(Mock laughter.)* I see! Ha! Ha! Ha! *(MADAM KOFO suddenly jumps to slap her. THE GUARD/ALAWO intercepts her hand in the air.)*

THE GUARD/ALAWO: E'joo Ma. Please!

MADAM KOFO: *(Furious.)* Your mother! Stay with whom? To spy on me? Yes, now I know. Your mother's spy. That's why you're always here. Ha! Ha! Ha! Today, it will end. *(Again, she lunges forward to slap SHAKARA, but THE GUARD/ALAWO is between them. They struggle.)*

SHAKARA: *(Panting.)* Dupe! Dupe! Dupe! Help! I'm dead! Help! Save me from her. Madam, please! Pleaseeeeeeeeese!

MADAM KOFO: For what?

SHAKARA: *(Chanting.)* Take me. I'm tired. I'm dead.

MADAM KOFO: *(Amused.)* Child, are you drunk?

SHAKARA: *(More passionately.)* Ma...Mommy, take me with you. I need...you...Oh, Dupe!

MADAM KOFO: Ahn no! Stop right there! Leave my innocent child alone. You people are so determined to spoil her...Ruin my poor baby for me. Eh?

SHAKARA: *(Interjecting.)* Oh no, Ma. It's...its only...you... You I want...

MADAM KOFO: Ohoooo! So it's me you want to kill?

SHAKARA: No Ma. God hears me. God will take care of you,

Ma.

MADAM KOFO: *(Relaxing in her chair.)* Don't 'Ma' me now. Get it? There's nobody here for you to mess up. The police will be here any time now. I've tried my best for your ungrateful mother. But that woman? She wants to challenge me? Ha! Let her come! Get ready! We'll see who laughs last! Ha! Ha! Ha!

SHAKARA: But Ma. My mother has nothing to do with this. In fact, I have no business with my mother. I have come to...to...you...

MADAM KOFO: *(Her countenance suddenly changes.)* To stay?

SHAKARA: *(Eyes light up.)* Yes, Ma!

MADAM KOFO: God, you heard me? Mo-dupe! Thank God, at last. *(She dances provocatively with THE GUARD/ALA-WO and SHAKARA admiring her.)* So you have heard my prayer? And what? Sheyi...Cynthia...no...ehm... em...what is that your name again?

SHAKARA: Shakara.

MADAM KOFO: Sha-ka-ra, your name? *(SHAKARA nods.)* Hnm...Sassy! Yeah, sassy! Bluff! That's it! That's the spirit! *(Pause, pulls her towards the sofa.)* Aha, Shakara my dear! Come with me. Alawo, get the phone. We don't need the police here. Not now. I was having such a bad day. But she's now brought me happiness. A bundle! *(She takes some provocative dance-steps, tries calling to cancel her order with the police.)* Yeye police. Their line is busy. Bastards! What can they do even? Imagine if someone had attacked me. I'd still be here waiting. And still, no help. Our police are so timid and so annoying too. *(To SHAKARA.)* Yes, my dear. So you have come to stay with me?

SHAKARA: Yes, Madam. *(MADAM KOFO hugs SHAKARA and sits her down.)*

MADAM KOFO: Come, my daughter. So your mother has now agreed that you come to see me for the business? I thought so. She's not an idiot, after all. I knew...I knew that she'd have to change her mind. Who likes to suffer? Who'd want to give up that kind of chance to better her life? *(She stares into SHAKARA's face as she caresses her hair.)* My daughter...

SHAKARA: Ma...Mommy. You see, I'm here on my own.

MADAM KOFO: You are?

SHAKARA: Yes, Ma. I have never agreed with my mother and sister on anything.

MADAM KOFO: And you don't have to, if they're so back-ward.

SHAKARA: I believe that we can change our destiny by our-selves. By...by being...

MADAM KOFO: Yes!

SHAKARA: *(Reciting.)* "Nobody has any reason to be poor in this rich country. We must look ahead."

MADAM KOFO: Yes! I mean...I was once like you. We all must struggle to improve our condition.

SHAKARA: "Use our heads...And change our world!"

MADAM KOFO: *(Jubilant.)* Yes! Come, my dear. Let's start loading up. *(SHAKARA obeys as her partner kisses the bags, chanting.)* "My precious bundle. My holy seed."

SHAKARA: Mommy, I'll do anything.

MADAM KOFO: Yes! Yes! Yes, me dear! Tell them! See mon-ey sitting there? *(MADAM KOFO shows her the heap of drugs. Next, she takes up the telephone and dials the phone.)* Hello, dear! My Chief Chairman! I told you. Trust me. I told you that it's only a matter of time. It will be done. And it's done. The girl is here. Her mother rejected the offer, but the girl is here. Brave young woman, I should say. And you know her name? Sassy! Sha-ka-ra! Yes, sassy! And you should see her. Really saaassy! Soon, I'll be handing her over to you. Yes, she's already loading up now. We'll be ready in no time. Expecting you soon.

SHAKARA: *(Lifting a bag.)* Mommy, where do I go now?

MADAM KOFO: Hnm...wait. Somewhere...somewhere...

(Pause.) Yes, there, my dear! You have the answer, my dear child. I wish Dupe could hear you now. *(Pause.)* Where is she anyway?

THE GUARD/ALAWO: Not back yet.

MADAM KOFO: *(Hissing.)* Foolish girl. Don't mind her. Alawo, come. Play that music. Then call me the driver. I'm ready to go now. *(The GUARD/ALAWO turns on the cassette player in the security post. With SHAKARA following, MADAM KOFO steps into the hot dance movements as they both stack up the bags, while THE GUARD/ALAWO amplifies the bass accompaniment with his security baton.)*

SHAKARA: *(Hauling bags.)* So Mommy, what next? Where do you say I'm going?

MADAM KOFO: *(Still loading up.)* Girl, out of this hell. Abroad. To God's own country. Now. Right now.

SHAKARA: *(Excitedly.)* Me? Abroad. Oh, Mommy! Teach me! Teach me what to do. What to say. I'm ready! *(MADAM KOFO demonstrates to her how to greet and carry herself like a lady; a business woman.)*

MADAM KOFO: *(Demonstrating.)* And you shake hands like this. *(They laugh as SHAKARA tries and fails.)* Remember, I won't be there. You're completely on your own. Use your head. Use your sense.

SHAKARA: *(Ecstatic.)* Yes, Mommy! Thank you! Thank you Mommy! *(As SHAKARA lifts the next bag, MADAM KOFO throws her last bag into the pile. She dusts and cleans off her hands, and goes to sit on the sofa.)* Child, I'm done. It's over to you now. I need to rest. I want peace. From now on, you hold your life right in your own hands. You alone will have to bear it to safety. Come, my dear. Follow me. *(Suddenly, the shrill sound of a car honking at the gate. It's "The Beast." The CHIEF CHAIRMAN enters. MADAM KOFO kisses him.)*

CHIEF CHAIRMAN: *(To SHAKARA.)* Great girl! Great girl!

SHAKARA: Thank you, Sir.

CHIEF CHAIRMAN: It's your type we need to move things in

134

this world. Turn the world around.

MADAM KOFO: Yes, dear. Absolutely.

CHIEF CHAIRMAN: Are you ready?

MADAM KOFO: *(Whistling the tune in the background.)* Yes, my dear. All set. Everything is in place.

CHIEF CHAIRMAN: Okay then. The driver is on his way. I'll take just a few bags now, in my own car. Packaging. That's most important. See you at the Airport Boarding Gate. *(Hugging them.)* Goodbye, my love! *(Kisses. They exit. The music is still playing in the background. The GUARD/ALAWO, alone, briefly takes over the stage and does some hot rap music "bata" dance steps, "Atilogwu" or some frenetic movements. He sees them coming and retires to his corner. They start counting the loaded bags in the vehicle. The music is now fading away and is replaced with the sound of a car behind the scene. The dogs start barking. Suddenly, another vehicle is heard screeching to a halt in front of the gate. It is the police van. Three armed policemen in combat uniform storm into the scene. The CHIEF CHAIRMAN, now masked, plays the role of the CHIEF DETECTIVE POLICE OFFICER or the DPO/SHANKA. The other two POLICEMEN are played by the CITY HOODLUMS. The GUARD/ALAWO has joined the Police team.)*

POLICE MAN TWO: There they are! Robbers!

POLICE OFFICER/SHANKA: *(Ready to shoot.)* Surrender! *(They freeze.)* Hands up! *(They obey. Sounds of dogs barking in the background. SHAKARA is trembling. At first, MADAM KOFO puts on a courageous front until the POLICE MAN TWO starts to interrogate the 'suspects' while the superior officer, DPO/SHANKA inspects the premises. The dogs' insistent barking signals to him the direction of his search. He's now drawn to the bags of weed. MADAM KOFO tries to hide her fears and attempts to distract the detective.)* You're Madam Risi Kofo, I take it.

MADAM KOFO: *(Bluffing.)* Yes. And what can I do for you?

POLICE OFFICER/SHANKA: Nothing, Madam. Just your guests

from the State.

MADAM KOFO: State guests? What for?

POLICE OFFICER/SHANKA: Checking. Just responding...

MADAM KOFO: But I don't need your help anymore.

POLICE OFFICER/SHANKA: Madam, we're here on national assignment. For protection.

MADAM KOFO: My protection? But I already cancelled the order.

POLICE OFFICER/SHANKA: *(Inspecting.)* I know. But we just have to be sure.

MADAM KOFO: *(Showing the door.)* In that case, thank you. And goodbye. I'm just getting ready to sleep. *(She slams the door.)*

POLICE OFFICER/SHANKA: Okay, Madam. Easy! Take it easy. There will be plenty of time to get worked up. As my father used to say, "there will be enough sleep for the dead man in the grave."

MADAM KOFO: So now what do you want?

POLICE OFFICER/SHANKA: Your cooperation. *(Showing his ID.)* Detective Dogo, Sergeants Bamfo, and Ofege from the Anti-Drug Squad. *(Showing her the search warrant.)* With orders from the headquarters to search your premises.

MADAM KOFO: What? Operation Sweep? *(She checks herself, adjusts her position and grins.)* Well, how's my beloved friend...your boss, Chief Commissioner Zombie?

POLICE OFFICER/SHANKA: *(Business-like.)* Very fine, Madam.

MADAM KOFO: *(Smiling.)* Oh dear! My dear, dear Chief. He's working too hard. He can't keep track of his men, straying...I mean, does your boss know you're here?

POLICE OFFICER/SHANKA: *(Sternly.)* Madam, mind your language! Nobody's straying here. Except you, perhaps. I told you already that we have orders from the headquarters. If he's the boss, then we're following his orders!

MADAM KOFO: *(Grinning.)* What? He knows? And he sent you? Are you sure he sent you here? This is Madam Kofo's Villa, you know. A highly respected society...

POLICE OFFICER/SHANKA: Look here, woman! Don't waste my time. I'm only a servant of the law. I obey orders. If you have questions, ask him, the boss—since you know him so well. For now, let me do my job. As an officer, I'm paid to find answers to nagging questions. As a citizen, your duty under "Section 1, Subsection 3 of the Penal Code Law" is to answer every question from any law enforcement officer. Right?

MADAM KOFO: *(Smiling. scratching her head.)* Right, Officer! You must be new on the job. Take it easy or you'll soon get burnt out.

POLICE OFFICER/SHANKA: Very well, thanks. *(Moving towards the bags as the dog continues barking.)* I can see you're traveling. *(No answer.)* Anything to declare?

MADAM KOFO: Nothing. Nothing to declare. *(Smiling, offering him a drink.)* Officer, you work so hard. And in this heat? Have a drink. Let's go inside and talk.

POLICE OFFICER/SHANKA: *(Turning, inspecting the bags.)* Madam, I'm okay. But thanks anyway. I said, anything to declare?

MADAM KOFO: *(Seductive, but nervous.)* Officer, I said have a drink on me...I mean anything. I'll be too glad to give...just anything to make you comfortable.

POLICE OFFICER/SHANKA: *(Sternly.)* And I said no! Thanks! Now, what do you have in these bags?

MADAM KOFO: *(Coughs, stammers.)* Ehm...nothing...Just the maid's...baggage...I mean...kid stuff...

POLICE OFFICER/SHANKA: I see. *(Examines the bags again, counts.)* Drugs. Cocaine. Exhibit number one, two, three...four. Indian Hemp Marijuana! *(Military command.)* Madam Kofo and Company! You're charged with seven counts of felony for the possession of dangerous drugs prohibited under the Federal Penal Code Law Number Z-100 Section National Emergency –Sub-

Section 911. Understand? *(Silence.)* Sergeant!

POLICE MAN TWO: *(Saluting.)* Yeessaap!

POLICE OFFICER/SHANKA: Arrest the suspects!

MADAM KOFO: What? Officer?

POLICE MAN TWO: Yeessap! *(Moves quickly, chains them amidst SHAKARA's sobs and MADAM KOFO's loud protests. The POLICE MAN TWO takes pictures of the crime scene.)*

POLICE OFFICER/SHANKA: Sergeant, start boarding up the house. *(POLICE MAN TWO obeys all orders.)*

MADAM KOFO: What? My estate?

POLICE OFFICER/SHANKA: Government...I mean, the people's property!

MADAM KOFO: *(Hysterical.)* Liaaaar! Rooooobber! *(Both suspects now in chains.)*

POLICE OFFICER/SHANKA: As you like, Madam. I only execute the law. *(Reciting.)* Under Decree 5, Section 419, 'The possession of drugs is dangerous and prohibited by law. Anyone and any premises found with drugs forfeits it automatically to the Federal Government for the public good and progress.' Nobody is above the law. *(Writing into his logbook.)* Therefore, this property, Number 23, Beach Haven is hereby seized under the Anti-Drug Operation Sweep. Henceforth, it will be used as a public property for community development.

MADAM KOFO: My sweat? God! Oh God of justice, where are you?

POLICE OFFICER/SHANKA: Here! Can't you see?

MADAM KOFO: *(Screaming, resisting.)* Nooooooo! This cannot be! Let me...let me go! *(Pause.)* Come, Officer. What do you want? Money? Jewelry? Foreign account? Or property? Let's make a deal. Anything! Anything you want.

POLICE OFFICER/SHANKA: *(Smiling.)* Thank you, Madam Generous! Your donation to the State will do just fine. Sergeant, start loading up. Quick! *(The Sergeants pile* *up the loot, one after the other. Sound of the police van outside.)*

MADAM KOFO: *(Passionately.)* Please! Please. I don't want to go to jail. *(Kicking her purse toward him.)* Here, take. That's my Swiss account. Take. Take. I'll do whatever you ask. On my honor.

POLICE OFFICER/SHANKA: *(Amused.)* Madam, your honor? *(Pointing to the bags.)* Bagged into this? Haba, Madam!

SHAKARA: *(Still sobbing.)* Please! Pleeeeease, Officer!

MADAM KOFO: Have pity on me. On her. I mean, she's just... a child. Have mercy.

POLICE OFFICER/SHANKA: But Madam, you see. Just like you, my hands are tied. I can't...cannot. The walls have eyes...ears. Anything I do is subject to the law. And the same thing applies to you. Everybody. You abuse the law, you pay. Simple. So, Madam, rest. Rest. *(Calling.)* Sergeant, time is running out. Lock up. But first, the van. Move the other suspect to one corner to create more space for these.

POLICE MAN TWO: You mean the Chief Chairman Oleh?

POLICE OFFICER/SHANKA: Yes!

MADAM KOFO: *(Alarmed.)* God! My chief? Did you say the Chief?

POLICE OFFICER/SHANKA: Yes, the Chief Chairman Oleh. Or rather, Money-Miss Road. Nabbed! Ha! Ha! Ha! Your partner in crime. Got him red-handed at the airport just now. Before settling into his own suite, for life, he'll be escorting you to your maximum security lodge. You'll both be making love in Tokyo. Ha! Ha! Ha!

MADAM KOFO: Oh, God! My Chief! My God! *(Traumatized, she doubles over as SHAKARA sobs in her own corner.)* My heart! My heart! *(Chanting.)* Dupe, my Angel! Come back to me. Please cooooome! *(The POLICE OFFICER/ SHANKA yanks them forward. The struggle intensifies between MADAM KOFO and the law.)*

POLICE OFFICER/SHANKA: *(Barking.)* About turn! *(The sus-*

pects obey.) Now, that's more like it! More like it. Madam, the law is blind. Tight. And, like you, I wish I could untie...undo...*(Teasing.)* But, Madam. Ha! This mountain on your back is causing obstruction. Haba, Madam! How do you intend to move on by holding back the wheel of progress? *(Military command.)* Now, attention! Stay still! Your back to the wall. Madam Coke...Kofo. Which one are you? Time to go. Now! *(Commanding.)* Left-Right! Left-Right! *(Both SHAKARA and MADAM KOFO obey the marching order. MADAM KOFO's eyes dilate, darting here and there to find a way to escape. She gropes and staggers, then falls on the POLICE OFFICER. His mask falls off.)*

MADAM KOFO: *(Shocked.)* Sha...Sha...Shanka! So it's you?

POLICE OFFICER/SHANKA: *(Awkwardly.)* I told you. I'm only a servant...I serve the people. I'm paid to enforce the law. I cannot help myself.

MADAM KOFO: But, I thought we were friends.

POLICE OFFICER/SHANKA: Neighbors. Point of correction.

MADAM KOFO: Well, you led me to believe we were friends.

POLICE OFFICER/SHANKA: Well, I'm sorry. But please note: "All friendship ends where my job begins."

MADAM KOFO: So, what are friends for if not to protect one another?

POLICE OFFICER/SHANKA: You mean to cover-up? Haven't I done enough? Ehn? Don't let me...

MADAM KOFO: *(Hysterical.)* Shanka, stop! Why do you want to strip me naked before the whole wide world?

POLICE OFFICER/SHANKA: No, Risi. It's you who started it all. You made a promise, remember. We made a pact, remember? Ah, Risi, how can you forget so soon?

MADAM KOFO: I know. I know. I broke my vow.

POLICE OFFICER/SHANKA: Shame! Shame on you! What did you expect? For me to lose my job? Implicate myself for someone who has no room for another? Eh? Look,

Risi. People try to save others drowning and making every effort to swim out of the deep sea.

MADAM KOFO: But damn it! When you found me, I was only trying to swim out of the sea! Out of shame and poverty. And only you knew it!

POLICE OFFICER/SHANKA: So you know? *(Pause.)* It's people like you who ruin the country. Mess it up. If you were a true friend, you'd help to make my job easier. But no. My so-called friend does her best to make my job harder. And now she expects clemency? Ha! *(Pause.)* Shame! See another child that you have ruined? *(Pushes the suspects against each other. They groan.)* Silence!

MADAM KOFO: Where are we going?

POLICE OFFICER/SHANKA: To paradise.

MADAM KOFO: *(Resisting.)* For God's sake, where?

POLICE OFFICER/SHANKA: *(Smiling.)* Do me a favor and leave God out of this. Don't you think you've given the Old Man enough trouble already? Leave the Old Man alone, let him rest.

MADAM KOFO: *(Resisting.)* Hell no! Where are we going?

POLICE OFFICER/SHANKA: *(Loud laughter.)* Thou sayest. Welcome to the national net. I deserve to be congratulated, Madam. For casting my net far and wide. Very wide. And here I am with such a big catch. Henceforth, call me Peter: the fisher of wo-men. Got it? Any more questions? *(He yanks her hand with that of SHAKARA.)* Sergeant Olege, go board up everything upstairs. Sergeant Bamfo, return to the van. Stay with the chief suspect. A very dangerous criminal, if you ask me. Just like my woman here. *(He pulls her to a corner and smiles at her.)* Yes, my dear neighbor. While waiting, let's continue our chat.

MADAM KOFO: I see. So this is the end? *(She kicks at the vanity dresser. The fine China Wares come tumbling down and smashing. He records in his log-book.)*

POLICE OFFICER/SHANKA: I've told you. Take it easy. It's not the end of the world. Just another phase. Another life. Get ready. Thanks to me, you're going to enjoy this freedom behind bars...(*He pushes them towards the front door.*)

SHAKARA: (*Wailing.*) Mama-O! Mama-O! Come! Come and get me! Take me home! I'll listen to you now! I'll hear you now! You told me. I'm sorry! Mama! Come!

POLICE OFFICER/SHANKA: Shut up, you! You think this is the Gondola nightclub where you go to rot? You think I don't see you? (*SHAKARA bites her lip, sobs.*)

MADAM KOFO: (*Tearfully.*) My daughter! My daughter! Where's my Dupe? My poor child. How's she going to cope?

POLICE OFFICER/SHANKA: Don't worry about your daughter. She and I understand each other and I'm in charge here. I'll take care of her.

MADAM KOFO: (*Sobbing.*) Why? Why, Shanka? I'm not the first to try to get out of poverty. And I won't be the last.

POLICE OFFICER/SHANKA: Neighbor, why? Why have you done this to me? Made my job so difficult? Impossible? Reports about you already reached the headquarters long ago. How? The laborers you kicked out and others...

MADAM KOFO: (*Alarmed.*) What?

POLICE OFFICER/SHANKA: Yes, my dear. Air waves. Signals. Many signals. (*Showing her picture exhibits of her and laborers in the weed farm.*) Look, your cup was full a long, long time ago. Even though we've been arresting others like you, I endured. Do you know that I could have lost my job because of you? I've been covering up. Hoping that you'd honor your word. But no! You are deaf. You only hear the sounds of hard, hard currency. (*Teasing her by jingling coins in her face.*)

MADAM KOFO: Look, I had to survive. Just like everybody else.

POLICE OFFICER/SHANKA: And on top of all these, your own daughter comes....

MADAM KOFO: What? My daughter?

POLICE OFFICER/SHANKA: Yes. She came to me with my new boss, the Chief Commissioner. Right in the middle of our strategy session on cracking down the drug mafia. So, what do you expect me to do? Lose my job? For what? Your drugs? Your greed? For somebody who has no place in her heart for anybody else in the world? Ahn-Ahn, Risi? Don't you think you're asking too much of others, what you can't give?

MADAM KOFO: Yes, preacher, say it. I know. I'm in your hands. At your mercy. But tell me, where is my child? She's innocent...my Angel. What has she got to do with it? Leave her alone! Leave my Angel alone! Take me. Do what you will with me. But...but my child? What have you done with her?

POLICE OFFICER/SHANKA: Not me, Madam. Ask yourself. Search your soul.

MADAM KOFO: My God! They've taken my daughter! They've killed her.

POLICE OFFICER/SHANKA: Nobody else but you.

MADAM KOFO: *(Hysterical.)* So she's dead? Tell me! My Angel is gone? We only had a fight. Only a quarrel. *(Gasping.)* Tell me, whoever had a teenage child that never had a quarrel with her? Ehn? Am I the first mother to disagree with her teenager? *(Sighing.)* Ah, my life! *(She bends over, clutching at her chest.)* My heart...over...it's over. *(Pleading passionately.)* I only ask one favor of you, now that I'm still here.

POLICE OFFICER/SHANKA: I'm listening.

MADAM KOFO: Please, let me...let me...see my Angel. Let me talk to her. Just once.

POLICE OFFICER/SHANKA: I know she's on her way.

MADAM KOFO: *(Agonizing.)* Wheeeeeeeeeere? *(POLICE OFFICER/SHANKA blows his whistle. POLICE MAN TWO runs in, stands at attention before him.)*

POLICE OFFICER/SHANKA: Ready?

POLICE MAN TWO: *(Saluting again.)* All correct Sir! Just only to open the motor. *(MADAM KOFO is cursing under her breath. SHAKARA is now in another corner by the door, praying fervently.)*

POLICE OFFICER/SHANKA: It's been a very long day. Thank God, I'm done. It's over Sergeant, quick. Go start the van.

POLICEMEN: *(Together.)* Yes Saaaap! *(Silence as all the PO-LICEMEN go upstairs for their final inspection. Suddenly, a knock at the door. OMESIETE enters, looking quite frantic and pulling DUPE along. KECHI follows immediately. Except for DUPE, neither OMESIETE nor KECHI seem to notice that SHAKARA and MADAM KOFO are in chains. DUPE sees them immediately and recoils.)*

OMESIETE: *(Still frantic and unaware.)* Madam? I'm glad you're still here! Come see me, see trouble-O! Your daughter ran to me since. And she vows she'll never come back to you. *(MADAM KOFO stares at her, silently. OMESIETE sees the chains.)* What, Madam? I can't understand.

MADAM KOFO: *(Seeing DUPE.)* At last! Ah, poor baby...Poor baby! *(Tries to hold DUPE, but for the chains.)* Poor baby! Mama Kechi. Omesiete! Please, pardon. Take care of her, please!

SHAKARA: *(Chanting as she stretches to catch her mother's hand.)* Ma...Mother. Forgive me. I was wrong. I was wrong not to have listened to you. I am sorry, Mama. Mama. Kechi. Mama. Dupe. Everybody. Forgive. Pleeee-aaaase! *(OMESIETE grabs SHAKARA and holds her tightly onto her bosom and begins gently rocking her in her arms as she bites her lips. KECHI joins her and they encircle SHAKARA.)*

MADAM KOFO: *(Tearfully.)* My sweet Dupe! Forgive. For God's sake! Forgive...I'm done. *(Pointing to OMESIETE.)* Stay close...to her...to them... *(Dupe stands, stone-faced.)* Baby, please. Please, my Angel. I couldn't help myself. I was running.

OMESIETE: Running from what? From where? Madam? You

too? What happened?

MADAM KOFO: Life. Life. The Law. God...I leave it to God.

OMESIETE & KECHI: *(Together.)* Who? Who did this?

MADAM KOFO: God. I leave it to God.

POLICE MAN TWO: *(Descending quickly.)* Here! *(They see him and the POLICE OFFICER/SHANKA. Silence until DUPE sees the POLICE OFFICER/SHANKA and thaws out from her frozen state and swiftly kneels before her mother as she clings to her. MADAM KOFO removes her gold bracelet, ring and necklace and puts them on DUPE as they tearfully rock in each other's arms.)*

POLICE OFFICER/SHANKA: What is going on here? *(Silence.)* Who are these? *(Still silence. Turning to DUPE, only to find that she's now locked in her mother's arms.)* Dupe, but why? I thought...I thought you wanted...wanted...?

DUPE: *(Snapping at him.)* Wanted what? Just leave me alone, you liar!

POLICE OFFICER/SHANKA: *(Surprised, trying to pull her back.)* Ha! Ha! Ha! Me? Liar? Who lied? Dupe? What is this? What happened to you?

DUPE: You!

POLICE OFFICER/SHANKA: Me? *(He tries to touch her, but she rebuffs him.)*

DUPE: *(Spitefully.)* Go away, you devil! Liar!

POLICE OFFICER/SHANKA: Me? Devil? Liar? What have I done?

DUPE: Everything. You! You! See? See what you have done? You're responsible.

POLICE OFFICER/SHANKA: Of course, I know. I am responsible. That is why I'm...I've got to be here...to do...my job.

DUPE: Yeah, right! See now. It's your fault...All...Yes, you! You deceived me. Betrayed me...Everyone.

POLICE OFFICER/SHANKA: *(Stunned.)* Betrayed you? How? Ha! Ha! Ha! Wonders shall never cease! Didn't you come to me today?

DUPE: Yes!

POLICE OFFICER/SHANKA: *(Smiling.)* Then tell them. Tell your mother what you said right in front of me and my new boss.

DUPE: *(Tearfully rocking her mother.)* I'm sorry. Sorry Mommy. I didn't know...that it will all come to this. I didn't...mean it this way. *(Turning to SHAKARA.)* Shak. Mom. I'm sorry.

POLICE OFFICER/SHANKA: *(Fuming.)* Ha! So what did you mean when you lodged criminal charges...?

DUPE: *(Shouting to drown his voice.)* Lie! Mommy, don't listen to him!

MADAM KOFO: *(Stunned.)* What? Yes, tell me!

POLICE OFFICER/SHANKA: I have nothing more to say. Ask your innocent daughter!

MADAM KOFO: D...Dupe...you too? Mo Kwu! *(Delirious.)* My life is over. It's over! It's over! Dupe, you? You?

DUPE: *(Consoling.)* That's not what happened, Mommy. I was framed. He and the Chief-boss made me tell everything.

MADAM KOFO: *(Delirious.)* And so you did? Aye-O! Life! My own Angel has killed me. *(Pause.)* So tell me, what did you tell?

DUPE: Oh, Mommy! Please! Please! I didn't know. I didn't know they'd use it against you. I only...wanted to scare...get back at you. Do something to revenge. Just to let you know how it hurts. It hurts, Mommy. It hurts. Don't you know? But I didn't...never wanted to hurt you. Not in this way. But Mommy, I told you. I told you to stop. But you wouldn't listen. No, you parents don't listen to your children. You think it's only children who must listen and obey their parents? Ehn, Mommy? Don't I always hear people say that love is a two-way traffic? Well, Mommy, you hurt me so many times, and you knew that you were hurting me. You provoked me. You pushed me and pushed me to the wall until I had nowhere else to run. Didn't you know that I was at the end of my rope? Didn't you see how depressed and miserable I was? And what did you do, Mommy? Did you ever want to hear me? Listen to me? See things from my own side? Oh, Mommy, you knew I had nobody but you. But you abandoned me. Abandoned me to her, the nanny. *(Indicating OMESIETE.)* To the world and the TV to baby-sit me. Why? Because you were making money. Said you had to make money. And I was alone. Alone! So, Mommy, what was I expected to do? Search and search for whoever would love me and accept me. And I found a home in her...She was the only mother I knew. And you know it. Now, look where we all are now, Mommy. What do you want me to do? Say I'm sorry? I'm sorry-I'm sorry and forever...Mommy understand. Please! *(Turning to OMESIETE.)* Please, pleeeease help me. Help me beg her...Pleaseeeeeeeeeeeeeeee! *(She falls at MADAM KOFO's feet and clings to her, eyes turned to OMESIETE.)*

OMESIETE: Please, Madam.

MADAM KOFO: *(Delirious.)* Aye-O! My life. It's over! It's over. My baby. My Angel has killed me. *(Sighing.)* Ahn! Let's talk about pain. And hurt. Do you know? Children. Your mothers are not stones. No! Mothers are humans too. They bleed. Breathe and cry like you. Oh yes, they hurt! Just like you. Know it, children! Your mothers are not super-beings. They may not cry out loud, but they too have their pain. Oh yes, they do! *(Turning to OMESIETE.)* Ask her, my friend, Omesiete. She knows. She too can tell.

OMESIETE: My fellow woman. Don't ask me. Don't ask me to tell my story. I too was once a teenager. I too did it to my mother. Though I knew it all and wouldn't listen. Where should I begin? Where should I end? *(Pointing to the three girls.)* You are the story that mothers have. And need to tell. And can tell. That's all I can say for now.

MADAM KOFO: *(Still delirious.)* Ah, my fellow woman! Tell

them! Tell them! Ha! Ha! Ha! Do you know my hurt? Do you feel it? You think you're alone? Do you really know me? Where I'm coming from? You know my story? Well, my dear child, I'll tell you. The old woman who sucks her lips now too once sucked the milk in her mother's nipple. Let me unload my own pain. The pain that I've nursed and carried through life from the time I took the first wrong step, at your age. And you know what? That's why he, that man, Shanka got me cheap. For only he knew. But he kept my secret. When everyone else rejected me, he gave me shelter, until my baby was born...

DUPE: *(Leaps onto his chest.)* Uncle Shanka? You? *(He nods, holds her tightly.)* Oh my God! My God! *(Holding them together.)* Uncle...Uncle...Mother...Uncle. Thanks. Sorry. Sorry.

MADAM KOFO: *(To the man.)* Shanka. Forgive!

DUPE: But tell me, Mommy...Uncle Shanka. What exactly happened?

POLICE OFFICER/SHANKA: A long story that only your mother can tell.

MADAM KOFO: Can I? Should I?

POLICE OFFICER/SHANKA: Risi, it's up to you. Everything is now out of my hands.

MADAM KOFO: My people! Tell me who has not made a mistake in this life? And as a teenager? Ah, my Dupe! You ask for my forgiveness? I ask for yours. Like you too, I have made my mistakes. Serious mistakes...which only that man, Shanka, knows. But I cannot say that he didn't try. Yes, he tried for me. To save me.

DUPE: Mommy, how?

MADAM KOFO: *(Stepping into the audience.)* I was in my second year in secondary school. We were poor, very poor. But my mother was most determined to send me to school. She tried everything to raise the money. Even selling her own clothes. But I fell in love with this teacher. Often, I'd sneak out of school to go and see him. Then, it happened; I became pregnant. Somehow, my mother suspected it. Tried to find out the truth from me. But I lied. Lied to my mother until it was too late. How long can anyone hide a pregnancy? Like a volcano, it soon erupts. Nothing you can do to hide it. But I tried. At first, wearing huge belts. Large sweaters. But nothing worked to hide my shame. Then, the school matron found out. Her tongue? Radio-Wireless! Nothing which crossed her went unreported. In spite of my plea, the 'Wireless' broadcast me to the principal and the entire assembly. Who made me pregnant? Taboo! How could I say it? My teacher? Never! I wanted to save him. His job. His family. I needed his help too. *(Pause.)* But then, he denied me outright! When I told him I was missing my time for six months, he simply laughed in my face. I still remember him making fun of me. *(Moves closer to the audience, starts play-acting.)* "You lost your time? Go find it! I don't have it, do I? Ha! Ha! Hey, guys! Now judge. My girl's miss...missing her...her you-know-what? Now she wants me to help her find it? How does any guy take or hold any girls time? Ehn? Guys, I can't understand it. She's dreaming. Must be dreaming, like them! Ha, woman? A trip! A sweet trap too! Girl, if you lost your time, go find it and leave me alone!" *(Pause.)* That was it. What choice did I have? Run back to my parents, and I did. But my parents were so disappointed they drove me out of the house. Told me I must go live with whoever was responsible. 'I sent you back to school to learn,' my mother screamed. 'Not to bring me back babies. You're a failure! A failure! You disgraced me. Now, I'm the laughing stock of the world!' she cried. 'Others go to school to bring back knowledge, mine goes to school to bring back babies!' My mother was in so much pain. I couldn't bear to see her that way. I ran away. Then changed my name and swore that I would never marry any man. I never wanted anything to take me back...remind me of that past. Since then, I've never been back home. Never! I was determined to prove them wrong.

Wipe out my past. A false-start. My first luck? I worked as a maid for the wealthy wife of this law officer. She'd made it big. Very big in the drug trade. Before too long, she mobilized me. Appointed me her agent and courier. And I proved myself. I had to. Fearless. Determined. I could fly everywhere. It didn't take long at all. One, two trips, maybe. Then I hit it. Big! That's how I made it. That's why, today, I can't stand weaklings or poverty. For if I could escape poverty, everybody else can. And should. There are many roads to life. Some very smooth. Some rough. Some safe. Some risky. Very risky. It's everyone's duty to choose. And I chose my path. Risky though it may seem. I was determined to make it, and succeed at all costs. But look where it's landed me today. *(Pause.)* My daughter, you made your mistakes. I, too, have made mine. So, how can I blame you? Forget. Forgive. *(They embrace.)*

DUPE: Mommy, now I understand. I didn't mean anything. I was only angry.

POLICE OFFICER/SHANKA: *(Entering.)* Young woman, one of the first rules of growing up is "Learn to manage your anger." Next, "If you don't mean it, don't say it." And then, "If you don't know it, don't tell it."

DUPE: But you alone knew better. Why did you give her up?

POLICE OFFICER/SHANKA: Yes, my 'General.' Your word is my command. I'm paid to serve you, am I not? You gave me an order and I simply obeyed your order. And here we are. So why do you blame me?

DUPE: But you promised...You promised not to hurt her. You didn't tell me you were going to arrest her. And my best friend too? Now look...what you've done to her. To me. To everybody.

POLICE OFFICER/SHANKA: *(Smiling.)* Baby, think it over. *(Turning to MADAM KOFO.)* Madam, time out! Time up! The boss knows. And is waiting. The nation too is waiting.

MADAM KOFO: *(Weakly.)* Okay, Shanka. You're right and I'm wrong. I should have done everything to stay out of trouble and to protect you. Keep my word. Our pact. But...no one knows it all. Nobody has all the answers to life's problems. I became too desperate. Too desperate. So now, let's make a deal.

POLICE OFFICER/SHANKA: Yes. I already said it's up to you now. Make an offer. At least for her sake...Dupe.

MADAM KOFO: *(Weakly pointing to SHAKARA.)* Please, release that girl. I'm ready to go, alone. But please, let my Dupe stay here. Don't give up this estate. And that woman, Omesiete, she knows my child more than anybody. Please, let her stay to take care of her...I mean the girls. *(She is falling slowly.)* That's all...I ask...God... My heart...Angel...Angel...My heart. *(She is visibly in pain, doubles over. Delirious.)* I cannot...can't go to jail. No! I'm free! Free! Free! To fly high! Never down. Down. It's over. Dupe...It's over. Ha! Ha! Ha! Look...look who's laughing now! I'm babyless. The babyless mother! Laughing. Babyless-babyless-babyless. Riding-riding-riding the sea. Traveling-traveling-traveling...Ha! *(Weak, muffled voice.)* Take...take care...Take care...I got my boat. Ready to sail-sail-sail...sailing...sailing...sailing... *(She slumps to the ground, faints.)*

POLICE MAN TWO: *(Pulling her up.)* Too heavy, Officer! I need help. *(POLICE OFFICER/SHANKA bends down to give him a hand, but notices that MADAM KOFO is not breathing. They all panic.)* Sergeant, quick! First aid!

POLICE OFFICER/SHANKA: Hurry up! Water! Water! Water! *(He feels her body, his face sags.)* No use. She's gone. *(Sighs heavily.)*

DUPE: *(Echo.)* Mommy! Don't! Don't go! I love you! Mommmmmmmmieeeeee!

POLICE OFFICER/SHANKA: A long time. A very long day. Sergeant, release that girl to her mother. *(The POLICE MAN TWO unchains SHAKARA. POLICE OFFICER/SHANKA now turns to the girls.)* Young people! It's up to you now! *(The POLICE OFFICER/ SHANKA washes his hands. At*

151

the same time, a mournful tune of the flute, followed by drum-beats. DUPE's wailing shatters the entire neighborhood as they all circle MADAM KOFO's body in a dirge and ritual dance. The POLICEMEN join the ritual. The music and dance rise to a crescendo. Sudden blackout.)

ABOUT THE AUTHOR

Author of many award winning plays, Tess Onwueme has earned international acclaim as one of Africa's finest women writers. She earned her PhD from the University of Benin, Nigeria in 1987, following her Master's and Bachelor's degrees from the University of Ife, Nigeria in 1982 and 1979, respectively. After years of teaching in both American and Nigerian universities, in 1994 Dr. Onwueme was appointed Distinguished Professor of Cultural Diversity and Professor of English at the University of Wisconsin, Eau Claire, Wisconsin where she still teaches to date.

Her creative works include: *No Vacancy* (2005), *What Mama Said* (2003), *Then She Said it* (2002), *Shakara: Dance Hall Queen* (2000), *Tell it to Women* (1997), *The Missing Face* (1997), *Three Plays* (1993), *Legacies* (1989), *The Reign of Wazobia* (1988), *Mirror for Campus* (1987), *Ban Empty Barn and Other Plays* (1986), *The Desert Encroaches* (1985), *The Broken Calabash* (1984), *A Hen Too Soon* (1983), and the novel, *Why The Elephant Has No Butt* (2000).

Dr. Onwueme was born in Ogwashi-Uku, Delta State, Nigeria. She is married with five children: Kenolisa Onwueme, Ebele Onwueme, Kunume Onwueme, Bundo Onwueme, and Malije Onwueme.